PRENTICE-HALL FOUNDATIONS OF PHILOSOPHY SERIES

D1096402

Virgil Aldrich	PHILOSOPHY OF ART
William Alston	PHILOSOPHY OF LANGUAGE
Stephen Barker	PHILOSOPHY OF MATHEMATICS
Roderick Chisholm	THEORY OF KNOWLEDGE
William Dray	PHILOSOPHY OF HISTORY
William Frankena	ETHICS
Carl Hempel	PHILOSOPHY OF NATURAL SCIENCE
John Hick	PHILOSOPHY OF RELIGION
Sidney Hook	POLITICAL PHILOSOPHY
John Lenz	PHILOSOPHY OF EDUCATION
Richard Rudner	PHILOSOPHY OF SOCIAL SCIENCE
Wesley Salmon	LOGIC
Richard Taylor	METAPHYSICS

Elizabeth and Monroe Beardsley, editors

STILL LIFE WITH A JUG, *André Derain*

Philosophy of Art

PHILOSOPHY
OF ART

FOUNDATIONS OF PHILOSOPHY SERIES

Virgil C. Aldrich

Kenyon College

PRENTICE-HALL, INC. ENGLEWOOD CLIFFS, N.J.

PHILOSOPHY OF ART, Aldrich

FOUNDATIONS OF PHILOSOPHY SERIES

C

PRENTICE-HALL INTERNATIONAL, INC., London

PRENTICE-HALL OF AUSTRALIA, PTY., LTD., Sydney

PRENTICE-HALL OF CANADA, LTD., Toronto

PRENTICE-HALL FRANCE, S.A.R.L., Paris

PRENTICE-HALL OF JAPAN, INC., Tokyo

PRENTICE-HALL DE MEXICO, S.A., Mexico City

FOUNDATIONS

OF PHILOSOPHY

Many of the problems of philosophy are of such broad relevance to human concerns, and so complex in their ramifications, that they are, in one form or another, perennially present. Though in the course of time they yield in part to philosophical inquiry, they may need to be rethought by each age in the light of its broader scientific knowledge and deepened ethical and religious experience. Better solutions are found by more refined and rigorous methods. Thus, one who approaches the study of philosophy in the hope of understanding the best of what it affords will look for both fundamental issues and contemporary achievements.

Written by a group of distinguished philosophers, the Foundations of Philosophy Series aims to exhibit some of the main problems in the various fields of philosophy as they stand at the present stage of philosophical history.

While certain fields are likely to be represented in most introductory courses in philosophy, college classes differ widely in emphasis, in method of instruction, and in rate of progress. Every instructor needs freedom to change his course as his own philosophical interests, the size and makeup of his classes, and the needs of his students vary from year to year. The thirteen volumes in the Foundations of Philosophy Series—each complete in itself, but complementing the others—offer a new flexibility to the instructor, who can create his own textbook by combining several volumes as he wishes, and can choose different combinations at different times. Those volumes that are not used in an introductory course will be found valuable, along with other texts or collections of readings, for the more specialized upper-level courses.

ELIZABETH BEARDSLEY   MONROE BEARDSLEY

To Liselie

and all the people, young and old,
who have colleagued with me
for philosophy's sake

PREFACE

"I introduce here a slight observation which I shall call 'philosophical,' meaning simply that we could do without it." Paul Valéry's remark captures the spirit of the later Wittgenstein which has dominated the Anglo-American approach to philosophical aesthetics. It expresses also the feeling of the average thoughtful reader who is not preoccupied with puzzling philosophical questions of the more traditional sort. Such people will be happier when they get to the discussion of the materials and media of art in the second chapter, and from there on to the end. But the reader who exposes himself to the preceding "philosophical" considerations will not find them so "slight" or dispensable when he moves on to the subsequent closer examination of the arts and the logic of talk about them. He will prize the philosophical considerations for the advantage they give him as a *philosopher* of art, even in his intimate relation to this or that work of art. It is the aim of this book in philosophy of art to introduce the reader to the subject in this advantageous way, illuminating instead of disrupting his rapport with art—perhaps even assisting him into such a relation if he was at a loss before.

VIRGIL C. ALDRICH

CONTENTS

INTRODUCTION

A phenomenon, popularly speaking, is something that teases people into thinking about it. In this sense, there are phenomena of art. I could call them the data of art, but this expression does not feature whatever it is that generates questions. Yet, both phenomena and data are given. They are the starting points. The difference is that a phenomenon is a datum with a penumbra of questions around it.

What, then, are the phenomena of art? This seems to be a request for specimens or examples. Here are some. Consider the medium of a painting or a statue. You see it as something. You see something in the pigment or bronze; it is animated with an image. But the strange thing is that this is not owing to any transparency of the medium. There is no analogy with seeing something either through a window pane or even in a mirror. A mirror image is not embodied in a medium; it is curiously disembodied, quite unlike an image in art. Or if you insist that the mirror is the medium, then you must notice that the image is not related to the glass and other materials of the mirror as the mountain image in, say, Cézanne's "Mont Sainte-Victoire" is related to the pigmented canvas. This makes the mirror image an intriguing phenomenon in its own right, and it teases the epistemologist; while the opaque work of art, coming to life under the manipulations of the artist, becomes a phenomenon for the philosopher of art.

Connected with this is the phenomenon of the space of a work of art. Even music and poetry are voluminous in a sense, and the teasing question is, in what sense? A moving-van operator sees a work of art in terms of space and time properties that seem not to be compatible

1

with its space-time properties as an object of aesthetic experience. I have in mind such properties as flatness, depth, etc. The pigmented canvas is flat in one view, but you see a solid apple "in the picture."

These considerations present a phantom phenomenon that haunts all philosophies of art: just what is the work of art as an aesthetic object? Is it, in this capacity, really there confronting one, or is it an illusion in some sense? Does Othello really suffocate Desdemona? What is teasing about this is that both alternative descriptions can be, and have been, given, in view of obvious characteristics of the phenomenon. Which is correct is not decidable without a more sensitive examination of the key concepts involved in the statements and of the phenomenon itself.

Then there is the phenomenon of the curious way in which a work of art is like something or resembles it. This remarkable sort of similarity may be appreciated and confirmed without first looking at the work of art and then at what it represents, in a comparison. You must somehow or other see the thing represented as located in the art work, if the representation has any aesthetic status. This is certainly not the way in which one would see or confirm the resemblance between, say, a Chevrolet and a Buick of the same year's vintage. Moreover, artistic representation can, paradoxically, be achieved without there being in existence anything that is represented.

So another phenomenon presents itself, namely, how representation in art is to be distinguished from expression (its expressiveness) and how they are related. It frequently seems as if it is only the expressiveness that counts, under a strictly aesthetic consideration.

More than this, many works of art seem to depend neither on expression nor representation. These are the formal ones. In such cases, what gets expressed, if anything, is an acute question, while it seems obvious that nothing at all gets represented. So here the really hard questions about expression in art are driven home: is the work of art expressive of feelings only, may certain characteristics of things also be expressed, or can the latter be only represented? Moreover, there are many expressions of feeling that have nothing to do with art, as in the case of your neighbor giving you an angry look over the expensive new fence. The phenomenon of expression in art simply vibrates with the penumbra of questions around it.

Speaking of form: you encounter a bit of music or a painting for the first time, yet can say of it at once and unerringly that it is a Mozart or a Cézanne. Is it the form of the piece that enables you to do this? Or is it the style? What is the difference between these, if any? And the medium and subject matter of a work of art, this seems to fuse with the form and content of the art work, making it self-sufficient;

yet is it not precisely the subject matter that lies outside it and that the composition represents?

Connected with this phenomenon is the paradox of the artist's ambiguous relation to everyday life and its values. On the one hand, the artist seems remote from life, caught in the self-sufficiency of his works of art and not knowing how to live, really; yet, on the other, he seems to be more intimate than nonartists are with life, so that he can reveal its secrets. (There is the old adage: he could save others; himself he could not save.) This distance-proximity relation of the artist to the world is quite phenomenal. And it seems to be this puzzling sort of relation to his work of art that others must get into if they are to experience it for what it is worth as art.

So we get to the phenomenon of aesthetic perception, which has many subtle tentacles linking it with the other phenomena. Perception in some sense—over and above the subjective response, if this is to count at all—certainly seems to be involved in aesthetic experience, be it on the artist's part or on ours who behold his work. Of course, it will differ from the perceiving which is scientific observing, but without losing its own sort of objectivity. Without this, evaluative criticism would not be feasible. And it is feasible. What is puzzling about all this is that, though some such objectivity is presupposed, apparently with the implication that aesthetic quality is there in the art object, yet the best artists and the most authoritative connoisseurs will, while looking straight at it, disagree as to what is to be seen in it. This is the basic disagreement, and it is amazing in this connection how changing the title of the composition modifies its perceptible content. We need a philosophy of titles of works of art. Superimposed on this stratum of agreement or disagreement of descriptions and interpretations is the level of evaluation, where judgments of aesthetic excellence are made. Here, too, unanimity is not guaranteed even among experts, and this phenomenon teases us into a closer scrutiny of how value terms are used in art appreciation and criticism. Is it the function of these terms to refer to (or name, or describe) any qualities at all in the work of art? Curious answers have been given this question, answers spawned by the basic phenomenon of the way the artist and art critic look at things and what this reveals to them. With this mode of perception goes the appropriate mode of expression, and the logic of this is a real teaser, as is the logic of its critical assessments.

What complicates this question is the variety of the arts, reflected, for example, in the title of Paul Weiss's book *Nine Basic Arts*. Types of statements that make important sense in relation to some of them are inept in application to others. In view of, say, a Hindemith quartet or a Braque cubistic painting on one hand and *Moby Dick* on the other, a general answer to the question, what is art? is hazardous. And the question, asked in general terms to invite the general answer, now concerns mostly amateur philosophers of art. But surely there is something in common, some thread that runs through them all, making them of the same general kind? Of course; but the phenomenal thing about this is that the shared characteristic may be quite insignificant or unrevealing when it is detected—not at all what one was after in the pursuit of understanding of the arts. To use an old term, it does not turn out to be the essence. So one begins to wonder about the essence, whether it is a will-o'-the-wisp.

A final phenomenon is brought to mind by generality. A good work of art is said to be universally significant, and yet is quite unique inasmuch as it seems to be the occasion for as many different individual appropriations of it as there are individuals. In short, though it does not address us in the language of generalization, yet what it means seems universally true. This sense of "true" is as phenomenal as anything. It has suggested to at least one philosopher of art that a work of art—even a Henry Moore petrified figure—is a proposition, couched in a certain way.

There are other phenomena of art, but those we have mentioned will suffice. Plato noticed and remarked on the fact that some objects of ordinary sense perception tease us into thinking about them because they are phenomenal, puzzling. Unfortunately, he pictured this situation as containing nascent contradictions, and therefore to be transcended in favor of another kind of objects: the abstract, imperceptible, consistent objects of thought, corresponding to concepts. So, in one mood at least, he looked on art with disfavor because of its reliance on perception instead of conception. But the only philosophy of art that has a chance will dwell upon and among the perceptible phenomena of art without tearing and eventually annihilating their delicate tissues. This sort of scrutiny, and the theory that takes shape in this contagious intimacy with the phenomena, I call phenomenological. Let us turn to the phenomenology of art—a sort of descriptive metaphysics that will avoid reducing or elevating art to something it is not, and will avoid replacing it by something that more properly goes under another category. Of course, art has relations to all of these, but the fair philosopher of art will prevent such relatedness from too omnivorously devouring art and denaturing it in a sort of digestive metamorphosis that is sometimes honorifically called a rational reconstruction. Art has already suffered enough from such alleged explanations, as so many other delicate phenomena have, such as the impressions of common sense.

So we turn to the phenomenological scrutiny and account of the phenomena of art. Some hypersensitive phenomenologists have said that this involves only an illuminating verbal activity, not a theory— *keine Lehre, sondern eine Tätigkeit* (Wittgenstein). But a theory of sorts is going to emerge. It will be neither inductive nor deductive in the scientific way, but will make an exhibitive sort of sense, reminding the reader of certain things he already knows and assisting him to see them afresh in a way that shows him also how the key terms of the discipline are used.

AESTHETIC EXPERIENCE

1

The Issue   In talking about works of art, people will frequently say that they like one better than another, or that they simply can't stand it. These remarks are plainly about the speakers. They are primarily expressions of subjective responses, though one may infer something from them about the works of art in question if one is acquainted with the speaker; his tastes, his expertise in such matters, etc.

It is a little more relevant to characteristics of the art work to call it nice, charming, pretty, lovely, beautiful. But even these remarks also turn out to be expressions of likes and dislikes in many cases; and even where they are intended as statements about the work of art, they fail to characterize it. From the judgment or verdict that it is pretty, nothing follows logically as to any characteristics it possesses, except perhaps strictly in context, and even then only quite deviously or in no strictly logical way.

But when someone says of the art work that it is dynamic, or unified, or delicate, or warm, or formal, or economical, then obviously some sort of characterization of the work is going on, and this takes a certain perceptiveness, a noticing of something in the composition. Anyone who should respond to such remarks by, "That's the way it looks to you, but not to me," and supposes that this settles the matter, would fail to recognize the sense of the remark. One who is talking in terms of this third set of remarks is at least trying to be objective in some tantalizing way. He means to report something in the art work.

This sense of objectivity is tantalizing because it is countered by another sense of the very same statements—a sense sometimes called "literal." A spinning top is literally dynamic; a picture of one is not, even if it is realistic or has lines for direction and speed of motion, as in a cartoon. Anyone with normal perceptual faculties can see and feel the dynamism of the spinning top. He is careful not to clasp it in the hurtful way. But he may be unable to perceive the characteristic in the picture or poem or bit of music that is *its* dynamism. Again, anyone who can see at all can see the unity of any picture, namely, that it is one picture. The combination of elements is, after all, one and only one combination. This is the literal unity. Clearly, a work can be characterized as warm, formal, or economical in the same way; all these adjectives can be used literally. Later, I shall treat "literal" critically, since a better word is available.

He who touches irons, sees and feels shapes, etc., can, out of such experiences, objectively characterize anything this way as warm or formal. But this bypasses the aesthetic characterization. Colors, contours, sounds, and combinations of these elements may be economical or warm in another sense—a sense that is also objective, with a view to characteristics of the object, in this case the work of art. Objective, yes, and using the same terms, but not in the same way. This brings the problem into focus.

It seems, then, that there is a mode of perception that is peculiarly aesthetic, about which much will have to be said. Of course, we may be objective in various ways, and some of these ways put perception as a whole in a quite subordinate position, as in systematic thinking about a subject (nuclear physics, e.g.) or in pure mathematics and formal logic, which have no factual subject matter at all to be perceived at any turn. Such conception too may be objective, meaning only that it is in accordance with rules. But it will simply not do to suppose that experiencing art is primarily an affair of thoughtfully interpreting things. It is basically perceptual. The kind of objectivity here in view will be fundamentally an objective way of looking at things, not of thinking about or interpreting them, though this will naturally attend the experience, elaborating it. The problem, then, is to distinguish experience of things in the aesthetic mode of perception from experience of things in the perceptual modes that ground nonaesthetic characterizations. In doing this, it will be a fatal mistake either to get away from perception *in toto* or to suppose that basically there is but one way to take a good, objective look at things; namely, the way that presents things as they literally are, the language of which we learn first and on which the subquent aesthetic uses of language are supposed to be "parasitic." Our talk in aesthetic terms may be parasitic or may depend on some basic mode of expression, but this is not going to turn out to be the literal one in rapport with, say, things as "physical objects."

Our problem, then, is to state the conditions to be satisfied by the sort of perceiving that is properly called aesthetic, the sort that reveals aesthetic characteristics of things. This is different from the question about the conditions which the thing itself must satisfy—whether it is a work of art or just anything—if *it* is to have such characteristics. The latter question will concern us in Chapter 2.

It will help us to start by placing the concept of aesthetic perception in a setting of the philosophy of perception in general. This will have the advantage of showing us where we are on the general map of philosophical problems of perception, as philosophers of one of its modes, namely, the aesthetic.

A sort of skeletal model influences or haunts much traditional and current thinking on the problem of perception. The picture is of a field of experience in which the subject (mind) confronts the object (matter). Both subject and object have a core or essence. What is essential or closest to the subject—in its mind—is its thoughts; then come feelings and sensations, moving outward in that order. The thoughts are quite inner and private; feelings are less so, and sensations are least so. You can guess what sensations the subject is having by looking around at the external environment, but you cannot thus guess its inner thoughts. For the object in the external world, on the other hand, the essential or closest thing is the physical space it occupies, because it is a physical object; geometry and physical science get at that essence, which is imperceptible. It has other less essential properties, still imperceptible or accessible only by scientific analysis. Least essential to it are its observable properties, which are linked with the sensations of the subject observing it. This connection with something subjective makes observable properties least essential to the object.

Here is a chart illustrating this picture of the field, a picture of "Cartesian dualism," for which Descartes is famous.

The Field

Mental (not in space)		Physical (in space)
Subject → thoughts → feelings	⋮	unobservables ← space ← *Object*
↓	⋮	↓
sensations ←	⋮ →	observable properties

Though famous revolts against such dualism have been staged right down to the present, the rebels have continued to be embarrassed by a difficulty pressed on them by this model when the question was: is aesthetic perception subjective or objective? The model leaves only one way to take a really objective look at things, namely, the perception that qualifies as observation; and this must be under controls that eventually purge it even of sensations or sensory impressions, as well as of feelings, if the point is to take the most knowing look at things. Thus is perception dissipated in favor of conception or thought. This is hard on aesthetic experience, which is reduced to nothing by such a purgation, since impressions and feelings are certainly integral to it in some way or other. So the tendency has been to admit the subjectivity of aesthetic experience and the notion that, strictly as such, it has no object at all, being simply an affair of expressing feelings, or getting the illusion of aesthetic objects, or involving a sort of double-talk about what really are physical objects only, "out there." Or one may turn the heat of this sort of embarrassment on scientific experience or observation and say that such observations are only of the subjective contents of the mind. We could say with George Berkeley that we really never get beyond impressions and images and feelings to a so-called external world outside the mind. Physical objects are nothing but regular clusters of sensations. Other idealists and phenomenalists have had recourse to similar alternatives that reverse the situation and bring the same sort of artificial embarrassment to bear on the notion of observational perception of physical objects.

The skeletal model responsible for these impasses has been in the closet of the philosophy of art too long. An adequate philosophy that will bury its ghost is suggested in this book, but our primary aim is to show the reader some philosophies of art and to equip him to be more conversant with, and about, the arts themselves. Still, this task will be undertaken in a framework of corrective and constructive suggestions that themselves jell into a philosophy—better, the phenomenology—of art.

But we should now turn to some of the various standard theories of the conditions under which perception becomes aesthetically relevant or revealing. The influence of the unfortunate dualistic model will be more noticeable in some cases than in others. The following brief notices of these theories will be worth much more if taken also as suggestions for supplementary reading.

Detachment and subjectivism   The ancient concept of detachment for aesthetic purposes is fundamentally the notion of getting out of gear with certain interests, so it is allied with "disinterestedness." But there are many versions of how this happens or how it is achieved, and what crucial interests are to be held in abeyance. The metaphysics in the background of the particular theory usually determines the account it gives of the detachment. If "metaphysics" is too strong here, then replace it with "beliefs as to what is true and real." This will take care of the possibility that science, without being a metaphysics, influences beliefs about reality.

If a scientific world-picture is the background determinant, then the theory of detachment for aesthetic purposes will emphasize the necessity of getting out of gear with the interest in truth and the objective way of experiencing that undergirds it. According to this theory, people dominated by this interest will, while under the domination, be blind to, or at least confused about, the aesthetic values of art. I. A. Richards has portrayed this state of mind in a famous formulation.[1] If the distinction is not made between truth and aesthetic adequacy, a common failure among religiously inclined people, some of the greatest works of art are made to suffer for it. They are eventually rejected as false when the scientific light dawns on them. For example, Dante's *Divine Comedy* presents a world-picture in conflict with the scientific picture. Even poetry, especially if it is epic, presents a scene in the field of the imagination, and this may be experienced—perceived, looked at, not just interpreted—in the wrong way for purposes of art. I remember a student who, in a humanities course, was annoyed at having to take Hamlet so seriously because Hamlet never existed in reality. His major interest was that of a scientific historian. To avoid this unfortunate jettisoning of art prompted by a wrong rapport with it, Richards argues that the function of art, properly conceived, is to organize the various subjective or psychological factors in the person having the aesthetic experience. This is to say that, strictly, it is not the job of art to reveal any characteristics of things at all—it would then compete ineffectually with science—but rather to do something valuable to the psyche of the person. So this turns out to be a theory, not of how to look revealingly at things, but how to lie in the sunlight of art for the inner health resulting from the exposure. One is supposed to let art produce a harmony within him.

Such subjectivism is common in the philosophy of art. It has liabilities, especially when introverted by the pressure of a scientific worldview, as in this case. It then fails to do justice to the notion of aesthetic *perception*, replacing this with the notion of some subjective condition. This tends to undercut objective criticism of works of art, or to embarrass it by requiring devious psychological considerations whose relevance to the question is controversial. And one wonders, in the theory's own terms, whether the impact of great art on the patient is to integrate him, inwardly or any other way, or instead to undo him in some sense. The greatest compositions tend to convey staggering realizations that

[1] I. A. Richards, "Science and Poetry," *A Modern Book of Esthetics*, ed. Melvin Rader (New York: Holt, Rinehart & Winston, Inc., 1960), pp. 270–85.

many people simply cannot stand. One would be left wondering what the evidence is for the possible countersuggestion that, in such cases, an inferior inner organization is broken up in favor of a superior or healthier one. Is this still an empirical hypothesis? If so, then there must be evidence to support it. Is there?

Subjectivism in the philosophy of art has considerable use for the notion of illusion. Subjectivism and illusionism tend to go together. There are degrees of subjectivism. I. A. Richards' theory is a fairly clear-cut case. Let us turn to some others that are not so clear cut, because they introduce the notion of objectification in some form or other—an objectifying of something that ordinarily is subjective but which, in the aesthetic case at least, seems to confront the experiencer as an object of perception. This puts more of a premium than the previous theory did on a right way of looking, not merely on a way of suspending belief. The brief mention that I shall give a few specimens of this sort of theory will serve the purpose, not of doing them full justice, but of setting the stage for the subsequent consideration of what I take to be a more adequate account of the phenomenon of detachment-without-loss-of-intimacy in relation to aesthetically experienced things in general and more specifically to works of art.

George Santayana [2] describes beauty as the feeling of pleasure objectified. This objectification makes the feeling appear as a quality of the thing being experienced as beautiful. Where such experience is educated into a critical and appreciative perception, there is perception of values of the thing as aesthetic object. Santayana gives an excellent account of how feelings usually function as motives for action guided by practical belief. Such perception bypasses the essence of things and expresses the active interests of the percipient in its transaction with what exists in the environment. But even feeling, as pleasure, can be put at a remove from its subjective seat where it prompts action, and can be made to appear as an essential quality of the object, in contemplative perception. The desire to possess the thing then vanishes, and one wants only to look.

This notion of beauty is at the disadvantage of failing to take care of the case of, say, a man desiring a woman because he perceives her as beautiful. Such cases force a distinction between beauty and aesthetic excellence, at least for one common use of "beautiful." This has been widely noticed by aestheticians, who have made various suggestions concerning what to do about it in theory. Moreover, a puzzling "as if" remains. Does pleasure, or any other feeling, really go out to qualify anything or to animate it? Either in the case of real lovers, or in the

[2] George Santayana, *The Sense of Beauty* (New York: Charles Scribner's Sons, 1936). Selection in *A Modern Book of Esthetics*.

picture-case of Modigliani's "The Two Lovers"? The latter pleases me. Does my feeling of pleasure as objectified really qualify the work of art? In reply to this, Santayana has some subtle things to say about the nonexistence of any essence as such, so that the question about what really happens in such cases can be made to look inept. But a less puzzling analysis of aesthetic detachment than this would help.

Bullough, in his well known essay [3] on psychic distance, also operates with the notion of a disengagement from subjective practical concerns and experiencing our own affections—usually subjective—not as inner motives to action but as objective characteristics of something outside. Yet he is wisely cautious about the use of the subjective-objective distinction in aesthetics. He warns us that it does not have the usefulness or even the sense it has in scientifically oriented discussions. Most accounts of art are only confused by introducing it. This insight must be developed later, for there is use for the subject-object relation even in philosophy of art, but under a special set of controls. Meanwhile, let it be conceded that when, on the strength of a scientific observation, the report of an aesthetic perception of certain characteristics of, say, a Barlach sculpted figure for a German cathedral is called subjective, something has gone wrong even though the report of such aesthetically perceived characteristics might well be subjective on grounds other than the scientific observation.

The detachment theme is given a dramatic variation in the theory of Ortega y Gasset,[4] which is ambiguous on the count of subjectivism and illusionism. He tells how one must take a stance that detaches him from lived reality in favor of a spiritual distance. Then one is in a contemplative rapport with something that retains a curiously ethereal sort of substantiality, a kind of "ultra-object" with its own set of specifically aesthetic characteristics. Then it is that expressive style and form become the dominant consideration instead of the representation of life values. A good composition will have some relation to lived reality, which is the condition of its being intelligible, but it will have as little resemblance as possible. Thus is human reality subject to dehumanization in art.

In the theory of empathy, whose best known expounders are Theodore Lipps and Vernon Lee,[5] the stress is again on the *self* as

[3] Edward Bullough, " 'Psychical Distance' as a Factor in Art and an Esthetic Principle," *Problems in Aesthetics*, ed. Morris Weitz (New York: The Macmillan Company, 1959), pp. 646–56.

[4] José Ortega y Gasset, "The Dehumanization of Art," *A Modern Book of Esthetics*, ed. Melvin Rader (New York: Holt, Rinehart & Winston, Inc., 1960), pp. 411–19.

[5] Theodore Lipps, "Empathy, Inner Imitation, and Sense-Feeling," and Vernon Lee, "Empathy," *A Modern Book of Esthetics*, ed. Melvin Rader (New York: Holt, Rinehart & Winston, Inc., 1960), pp. 370–82.

apparently feeling itself into (*Einfühlung*) the object of aesthetic perception. This is done in a kind of subjective enactment that apparently objectifies the activities of the self into the object. The statue, the mountain, "rises" out of its base. Lee goes so far as to say that science and philosophy have shown that such anthropomorphizing is not objectively warranted, but has its own subjective values, nevertheless. Aesthetic value is a kind of self-enjoyment, though involving an inner detachment or psychological distancing of the self from itself. The ghost of the scientific world-view haunts this way of thinking about aesthetic perception and confines the operation of aesthetic perception in order to protect the self from the incipient illusion in this way of experiencing things.

Before illusionism is discussed, I want to mention Aristotle's notion of catharsis under the head of subjectivism. I do this with some hesitation, however, because it can be shown that this concept is not simply a clinical one. At first blush, it does seem to be about a purgation, taking the poison out of, say, pity and terror as experienced in reality or action. But there are innuendos in Aristotle's thinking about the matter which suggest that this affair of (dramatic) art doing something good for the psychological health of the spectator is not its main value. Rather, we turn to art for a fuller, *contemplative* realization of the terrible and pitiful condition of human life. Thus do we come into a sort of understanding not only of the objectified emotions themselves, but also of the nature of the human enterprise in its cosmic setting. This understanding is "truer" than the sort that history and empirical psychology and sociology give us. Aristotle said so, among other things. I leave this interpretation in the lap of the reflective reader, to be spelled out in the light of the *Poetics*.[6]

Illusionism and phenomenalism

Worth dwelling on for a while is the most subtle treatment of the concept of illusion in relation to the experience of art, in a book by E. H. Gombrich.[7] What makes it subtle is that it features the wonderful, constructive power of imaginative perception over its object. In putting a premium on this, Gombrich is unlike Plato who, toward the end of his program of social reform as outlined in *The Republic*, associates the illusions of art with deliberate deception and so finds them vicious on moral and metaphysical counts. According to this Platonic vein (there are other, contrary ones in Plato) the skilled artist is a menace because he induces false beliefs about reality and stirs

[6] Aristotle, *On the Art of Poetry*, trans. I. Bywater (London: Oxford University Press, Inc., 1920).

[7] From E. H. Gombrich, *Art and Illusion*, Bollingen Series XXXV (New York: Pantheon Books, 1960). By permission of the Trustees of the National Gallery of Art, Washington, D.C.

up emotions subversive to reason in people. The nearest approach to such a view in modern times is Tolstoy's theory of art [8] as a purveyor of emotions, aiming at a community of feeling. This is why art is demoralizing if not kept under controls that make its emotional product simple, moral, and spiritual. Unlike Plato, Tolstoy holds up a community of such primitive, spiritual (preferably Christian) emotions as the end of the good life for man. So good art has a supremely important function, and such art as Shakespeare's gets a low rating—too sophisticated.

The contents of Gombrich's concept of illusion in art are sophisticated by the dual influence of science and of Kant's critical philosophy, which makes his concept a subtle variety of phenomenalism. Since we are here considering the aesthetic way of experiencing things, I shall try to isolate the remarks in *Art and Illusion* that bear on this, in distinction from its pronouncements on the *object* of aesthetic experience. The object will be our topic in Chapter 2.

In the first place, Gombrich cites many authorities in philosophy and psychology in support of the thesis that no mode of perception is primarily an affair of *beginning* with atomic sense impressions (sense data) and constructing its object out of these. He rejects that kind of phenomenalism. If anything is to be taken as simply given first and subsequently elaborated, the concept of an initial indeterminacy or ambiguity of the field of experience serves us much better; a not-determinately-formed milieu. This, subsequently, differentiates into the definite sort of perceptions we are conversant with and articulate about; and the real question is how this comes off. This was Goethe's question as to how the mind gives form to the indeterminate; the kind of question Kant tried to answer systematically, with the new natural science breathing down his neck. Leonardo da Vinci also noticed this phenomenon [9] —the creativity of the forms of imaginative perception playing on material that is wonderfully malleable under their action, as in looking at "certain walls stained with damp" or clouds or muddy water (quoted in Gombrich, *op. cit.*, p. 188) and seeing them as all sorts of things that can be captured and realized in a work of art. Gombrich treats this phenomenon as involving a making and a matching. For the making, the mind uses schemata or forms that provide the architectonic for the material of the experience. These, in a way, come first. When the mind is operating with such a structure, it tends to see it in things. In fact, things are the constructions resulting from the projection of forms into the material. This is the mind's elemental or primary constructive act, which presents a world of things for this or that sort of experience. Because these constructions are so far beneath the level of deliberate

[8] Leo Tolstoy, *What Is Art?* (London: Oxford University Press, Inc., 1938).
[9] Leonardo da Vinci, *Treatise on Painting* (London: George Bell & Sons, Ltd., 1897).

making by the mind, they may appropriately be considered as its findings—the purely visual figures, for example. But psychology books are full of such figures which, though found, are nevertheless liable to appear this way or that—Ames' chair experiment (p. 248), the staircase drawing seen from above or below, the black cross in a white field switching into a white cross in a black field. This reveals a bedrock ambiguity even in the most elemental perception and brings into prominence the function of the percipient's mental set that determines what he is going to see.

Given such constructions and their likenesses, the mind is tempted to move on to a matching operation in a representation of something. This is a secondary sort of construction that gets us nearer to artistic creation. The artist sees a form in something and proceeds to fill it in with a content or material of its own, detailing it into a likeness of something suggested by the form.

The point of Gombrich's excellent book is that representation in art is a tricky business, since it does not and cannot consist of copying, in the medium of the art, a wholly determinate and fixed original. Mental sets, either cultural or individual, are at work from the ground up. This is why representation has a history and why, in the final analysis, it is not sharply distinguishable from expression. The painter's eye, for example, is to be thought of as a mental set; this is what he sees with, the constructive organ of sight.

The nature and function of illusion, according to this theory of aesthetic perception, are hard to pin down. The author has intentionally left the concept of illusion in art ambiguous. In one sense, all art is illusory because there are no fixed models to copy. In another, since copying fixed models cannot be the standard of objectivity and realism in art, some works are nonillusory by another standard that is hard to formulate. Edwin Boring said that there is no illusion where there is no pretense of copying reality.

Gombrich, like Kenneth Clark, is impressed by the illusion involved in stepping back from a painted canvas and seeing it as a man or a mountain. Recent artists have been annoyed, he believes, by this phenomenon and the crippling demands it makes on art that would be purer without it. So they turn to abstract art that avoids representational construction to be rid of the illusion that is supreme in them. A cubistic painting, for example, forces attention on form and medium, leaving the illusion of representation out. Curiously, the works that have been called realistic are, by this standard, the most illusory. They depend on a kind of *trompe l'oeil* (eye-deception) for their effects, of the same sort that is more obvious and less controlled—and therefore aesthetically less valuable—in the ambiguous diagrams in the psychology books.

As for the aesthetic value of a work of art, Gombrich leaves us with the impression that this is the demonstration of the creative and expressive power of mind over its perceptual materials. And what the art work expresses or exhibits—the content of its expression—seems, in his account, to be primarily just this formative power of the mind. The ordered world of objects, more conspicuously in works of art, is thus shown to be a creation by mental sets.

I have taken time with this theory of aesthetic perception because it is a fine point of departure for the discussion of key concepts in the philosophy of art. We shall have occasion, later, to return to it in a more independent critical treatment.

In another well worked-out version of phenomenalism, the notion of illusion is much more restricted. This is because much less is made of the creativity of aesthetic perception. According to Beardsley's phenomenalism,[10] becoming aesthetically perceptive is mostly an affair of restricting one's attention to an aesthetic object that is a kind of perceptual object found in the "phenomenal" or perceptual field of sensible appearances. The only construction involved is that of the artist in the manipulation of his materials, the result of which is the work of art. The work then appears to the percipient as a special sort of phenomenal object.

The contribution of the mind or of the aesthetic way of looking at things is thus played down. Indeed, Beardsley severely demands that much be excluded from it—subjective feelings and considerations of the physical and psychological conditions of the aesthetic object. This is an excellent declaration of independence in favor of the objectivity of aesthetic perception, and some such stand must be made if objective evaluation of aesthetic quality is to be at all feasible. Without this, no impressions of the work of art could be called illusory or even just mistaken.

Yet, Beardsley says, "we do not come to the aesthetic object cold" since "our capacity to respond richly and fully . . . depends on a large apperceptive mass . . . which may include some previous acquaintance with the general style of the work." Thus the mind does contribute something via an experienced and otherwise educated perception. Until the looking is discriminating in this way, it is neither responsible nor aesthetic. "Illusory" qualities will befog the experience and lead to mistaken judgments, without such education.

Illusion in art is, in this view, mainly an affair of mistaking certain factors for characteristics of the work of art, factors which in fact are irrelevant to it as an aesthetic object. If you are a jealous husband, you will tend to see in Othello what is not there. Shakespeare's biogra-

---

[10] Monroe C. Beardsley, *Aesthetics* (New York: Harcourt, Brace & World, Inc., 1958).

phers will be similarly tempted to a failure in discrimination. Clearly this view makes illusion less pervasive and dramatic than that of Gombrich who is more kin to Kant.

But, still, there is a pervasive subjectivism in Beardsley's phenomenalism. According to him, there are really two objects wherever it is ordinarily thought that there is only one. For example, in the case of a chair, there is the physical chair and the perceptual chair. The perceptual chair consists of presentations given to sense. These are "appearances," and it is these which, with certain qualifications, figure as aesthetic objects. In technical philosophical thinking, any appearance strictly as such is a phenomenon; and so we get the name "phenomenalism" for any theory that features appearances. "What really concerns the critic [of a work of art] is its appearance," says Beardsley. And in a brief section on aesthetic experience, he describes such perception as a kind of make-believe, conversant only with the surfaces of things in an exclusive awareness that makes one wonder if we should think of its having any objects at all. Though such aesthetic experiences are more unified, intense, and complex than nonaesthetic ones, they involve a curious sort of illusion-without-deception that the percipient is confronted by something while actually he is not; he is not, that is, insofar as what confronts him is just an aesthetic object.

From here on Beardsley is hard put to do justice to his excellent demand that aesthetic perception be objective, since it is difficult, on these grounds, to determine how a set of immediate sensory presentations can constitute a single, durable aesthetic *object*. We shall consider this case, along with others, when we get to the consideration of things as aesthetic objects later in this chapter and at the end of the book. The final remark here is that the ghost of the possibility of systematic illusion haunts even this fine specimen of a phenomenalistic theory since, according to it, appearances are of the essence, on a basis of physical realities; and these appearances must be isolated from their physical bases by a selective sort of attention. In this respect, the notion of detachment still has some relevance and even force.

Notice of the famous depth-psychological and theological concepts of illusion will come later in connection with aesthetic interpretation.

Aesthetic experience without detachment or illusion The best way to establish the case against illusionism and subjectivism is to delete the notion of detachment and to stress the very opposite. Then, instead of getting out of gear with this or that factor, we will emphasize the wholeness of the perception, the sort of perception that is fairer than usual to the integrity of experience as a whole. Instead of isolation there is integration of elements. In this view of aesthetic perception, its role is to redeem experience from its ordinary dislocations, fragmentations, and bare mechanisms, either by disclosing the underlying organic unity of experience or by producing such wholeness through an intelligent ordering of the situation.

It is the notion of human agency, both manual and perceptual, in producing wholeness, that John Dewey has developed into a theory of art as a kind of experience.[11] Considering this theory after Beardsley's phenomenalism is appropriate because it has influenced Beardsley and, more important, it is the kind of theory of aesthetic experience that is left if the notion of physical objects as the underlying substantial correlatives of aesthetic objects (phenomenal appearances) is stricken out. Then, even perceptually speaking, we are really in the swim of things, where "things" now are the relatively stable presentations that congeal in the on-going current of ordinary experience. Nothing substantial is left down out of sight and in principle inaccessible to perception. That sort of dualism Dewey has nothing to do with. Thus, according to him, no detachment is necessary to aesthetic experience, no exclusive looking at things. So the sense of a rapport with their surface appearances in aesthetic perception disappears, together with the notion that they produce a quasi-illusion as a colorful veil covering imperceptible full-bodied things beneath.

If the experience is to have aesthetic quality, it must achieve not an exclusion of various factors ordinarily present, but an inclusion more comprehensive than usual, presenting a felt unity of the elements that appear more scattered in routine perception. Suppose, for example, that to produce a certain result, you do something. You may experience such an operation as a mere means to an end, and then you will not perceive it as an integral component in and of the final result. Perhaps this is the more usual sort of experience people have in the work-a-day world, and Dewey would minimize such fragmentation even there. But suppose it is a soup that an artist in gastronomics is preparing. This will involve delicate operations of adding and balancing ingredients, subjecting them to right temperatures for the right durations, and a studious tasting now and then. All this is under the pervasive influence of the end sought, which is the control on the operation. In short, such experience is cumulative and consummatory. The final partaking of the soup will, for the connoisseur, be a consummation in which the productive operation is felt—even tasted—as ingredient in the soup. The taste in this aesthetic case is what Bernard Berenson would call an "ideated sensation," not at all the raw sensation it is in the routine experience of one who hurriedly ingests the food as a mere means to sustain himself through the afternoon's business. Thus is aesthetic quality a felt unity of ends and means, making the whole experience

[11] John Dewey, *Art as Experience* (New York: Minton, Balch, and Co., 1934).

gravid with consummatory meaning, in which the "doings" (productive operations) are experienced in fusion with the "undergoing" (the consummatory phase of the experience). This sort of experience, in greater or less degree, one may have in work-a-day situations wherever it has something cumulative and consummatory about it. Coming out of such an experience, one naturally ejaculates, "That certainly was an experience!" Dewey features this sense of "an experience" in his notion of art as experience.

But it is the special function of the artist to provide people with occasions for aesthetic experience. So he produces works of art. These exhibit more clearly how integrated and meaningful experience can be. Their point is a sort of perceptual demonstration of the felt unity which, in routine experience, is usually too diffuse or thin to count for much. It is as if the artist manipulates his material in a way that makes the manipulation (the doing) a perceptible dynamic quality transfusing the finished work (the undergoing) in a fine demonstration of the unity of means and end. If this can happen with a finely wrought soup, how much more readily does it occur in media that address themselves primarily to hearing or seeing—the clay, say, of a well-wrought urn. This is perception heightened above the ordinary threshold of bare recognitions that serve practical purposes.

Here ends the exposition of Dewey's theory of aesthetic experience. This one specimen (Tolstoy's is another) of a theory of art without detachment or illusion is sufficient for our purpose. It is noteworthy that this attempt to keep art close to life has little use for the more popular notion of the way to accomplish this—by realistic representations. Dewey has a more subtle notion of how life-values are bodied forth in any materials and any forms that answer to the demand that aesthetic perception makes for a rounding out and integrating of experiences. In fact, his treatment of this takes the props out from under the concept of art as representation, and puts the emphasis rather on the sort of expressiveness that makes both aesthetic perception and its object a consummation of creative work.

Let us now attempt some constructive suggestions, and use them to arbitrate the dispute among the theorists mentioned previously.

A new formulation   The notions of the detachment, subjectivity, and illusion alleged to be characteristic of aesthetic experience, and the opposition to these allegations, have preoccupied us in this part of our study. I want now to conclude with some constructive suggestions that keep in view the phenomena that caught the attention of the theorists above, but by a treatment that, through corrective modifications, does greater justice to the key concepts of their theories. The phenomenology of art requires such procedure to avoid the wholesale rejections one is tempted to make by a reductionist or simply too exclusive way of thinking about the matter.

The stage is set nicely for my task by certain remarks in an essay by Frank Sibley.[12] His main concern there, the logic of aesthetic terms, will occupy us at the end of the book. But he mentions aesthetic "perceptiveness" as a special "ability to *notice* or *discern* things," distinguishing this from mere subjective preference or liking on the one hand, and from the good eyesight of people with 20-20 vision on the other. This kind of perception is precisely what I am trying to isolate and characterize for what it is worth. First comes a statement of the framework of my philosophy of art, the sense of which will be detailed throughout the rest of the book. It will help to have a general impression of it to begin with.

What suggested to me the following theory of aesthetic perception and required me to stretch the concept of experience is the phenomenon that intrigued Gombrich and Wittgenstein: the phenomenon of the change of "aspects" in the duck-rabbit picture, the staircase drawing, and the cube diagram. For example, look at this figure

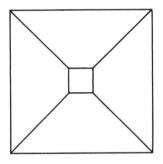

under these five titles: (1) square suspended in a frame, (2) lampshade seen from above, (3) lampshade seen from below, (4) looking into a tunnel, and (5) aerial view of a truncated pyramid. Call these "subject matters." You will notice that the space values of the figure are fixed according to which subject matter it is seen as. Call this a change of "aspects," and the phenomenon of the change itself "aspection." Although a condition of what you see is what you have in mind, the aspect is not just a thought or even just a subjective image; it is an object of perception of some sort. The figure objectively accommodates the various aspects.

That this is *not* so is suggested by the notion that the figure really or in itself is a physical object. So we get the notion of the projection

[12] "Aesthetic Concepts," *Philosophical Review*, LXVII (October 1959), 421–50.

of images that are only apparent, and thus of perceptual illusion. This is because the shape of a physical object does not change under aspection. Physical objects do not objectively accommodate aspects.

But reconsider the figure with a view to what it is simply or in itself. In the first place, you will find it difficult to get such a basic neutral awareness of it. It more readily appears as this or that. But, if pressed, we can report that what is simply there is a figure in printer's ink on white paper, the space values of which are indeterminate or not definite without presuppositions or ways of looking.

You may retort that anyone can see that it is a physical object. Well, what sort of seeing is *that?* Do I *simply* see it that way? I *can,* of course, see the figure as flat on the surface of the page and perhaps the page itself as a flat physical object, but this is an educated perception appealing implicitly to a standard of physical flatness. To see it that way is an achievement. You don't *simply* see it that way. In fact, I find it difficult to see the figure as flat on the page, but quite easy to see it protruding or receding in a white field as a lampshade or a tunnel. And to call it a physical object raises age-old questions as to whether it is visible at all. Physical objects are not simply seen. They are observed, and observation is under controls. Ask the scientist, if you distrust what philosophers have said about this.

Anyway, I shall say that what is simply there is a determinable somewhat—a figure in printer's ink on white paper—and shall call it, certainly not a physical object, but a "material thing." "Material" here suggests a potential for this or that formulation, perceptual and conceptual. This is the phenomenologically innocent use of "material." (Look at "matter" and "material" in these uses: "What's the matter?" "That's immaterial to me"; "Let's sit down and discuss the matter"; "That's material for a court-case"; "Can't a more interesting subject matter be found?" And think of Aristotle's use of "matter" for the potentiality of a thing's becoming this or that, realized in this or that form.) It is a use free of presuppositions, whereas "physical object" and "aesthetic object" are not, but are categories under which the material thing is realized as an aesthetic or physical object. "Thing" here is also an innocent word, unlike "object," which presupposes a category and a way of looking—a mode of perception.

What I am approaching is the phenomenon of categorial aspection. It is so pervasive that it usually escapes notice. The same material thing may be perceptually realized either as a physical or as an aesthetic object. This refers to two modes of perception different in category. In the figure above, on the other hand, it was an affair of seeing the material thing (the figure) as a number of other things. Categorial aspection involves a change of categorial aspects; the same material thing is perceived now as a physical object, now as an aesthetic object, neither of which involves seeing it as another *thing*. The difference between categorial aspects has to do with modes of perception and the kinds of space [13] in which their objects are realized. Moreover, such aspection is not as much under voluntary control as is the lampshade sort, since it involves an educated looking which is a gradual achievement.

Let us call "observation" the perceptual mode in which material things are realized in physical space. Then the very looking at things will be an incipient awareness of their space properties as fixed by metrical standards and measuring operations. Things seen this way will have a different structural cast from that of the same things in the aesthetic perception of them. Let us call the latter mode "prehension." The aesthetic space of things perceived thus is determined by such characteristics as intensities or values of colors and sounds, which, as we shall see later, comprise the medium presented by the material things in question. Take for example a dark city and a pale western sky at dusk, meeting at the sky line. In the purely prehensive or aesthetic view of this, the light sky area just above the jagged sky line protrudes toward the point of view. The sky is closer to the viewer than are the dark areas of buildings. This is the disposition of these material things in aesthetic space with respect to their medium alone. It is precisely the medium in this sense that is discounted both in the observational view of them and in the plain, nonspecial view. Thus prehension is, if you like, an "impressionistic" way of looking, but still a mode of perception, with the impressions objectively animating the material things—there to be prehended.

Let us say, then, that under observation, the characteristics of the material thing are realized as "qualities" that "qualify" it, while for prehension, its characteristics are realized as "aspects" (objective impressions) that "animate" it. Such animation will occur in two ways or senses: (1) in the prehension that involves getting the aesthetic space-values of the thing as structured simply by color and sound; this is, simply to see a material thing as an aesthetic object, a case of a categorial aspect—the sky line above is an example; and (2) in seeing the thing as something that it is not thought really to be; the figure is not mistaken for a lampshade while it is being seen as one, but it is animated by the image of something else. Representational works of art feature this second kind of animation. Both sorts of aspects or animation occur without any change in observable qualities of the thing as a physical object.

The presuppositionless terms in this account are: (1) "thing,"

[13] Virgil C. Aldrich, "Picture Space," *Philosophical Review*, LXVII (July 1958), 342–52.

which here specifies into "physical object" and "aesthetic object;" (2) "perception," which ramifies into "observation" and "prehension;" and (3) "characteristics," which are actualized as observed "qualities" that "qualify" the thing, or as prehended "aspects" that "animate" it. The presuppositions of the various controlled ways of looking at and talking about things are formulated in the categories specified for "physical object" and "aesthetic object," for "observation" and "prehension," and for "qualities" and "aspects."

A final crucial point: the distinction between "physical object" and "aesthetic object" is not anything like the distinction between "material" and "mental." Any object is a material thing appearing one way or another. There are no mental objects, fundamentally speaking. Materialists and idealists in metaphysics have concurred on this. But the point is that as "object" is a category word with presuppositions—physical or aesthetic—so is "subject." The diagram below illustrates it, and, in our thinking about art, should replace the unfortunate one given before on p. 8. It is a picture primarily of categorial aspection.

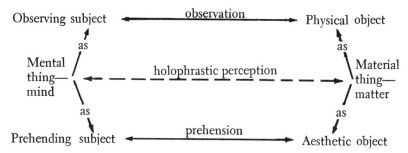

The message of this is simple enough, and is of tremendous importance for art. It means that the mind, as a potential for this or that sort of experience of material things, does not necessarily become subjective when it gives up observing them. The notion that it does become subjective was the unfortunate result of the traditional unilinear model. There is another access to material things—as objective in its own way as the observational is in its way—that the mind may take as prehending subject. In such a rapport, the things will be realized as aesthetic objects, in the prehensive mode of perception. But since perception in either of these two determinate modes is an exclusive achievement—one excludes the other—a basic simple perception of things is presupposed, in the swim of which both material things and mental things are determinables, not realized as definitely this or that sort of objects and subjects. "Mind" and "matter" are therefore limiting concepts in the direction of polar opposites beyond categories. The non-special field of their fundamental rapport I call "holophrastic," a word that suggests something in which much is compacted both in that non-special kind of perception and in its nonspecial mode of expression in "ordinary language."

But you will not digest this scheme of concepts without the help of the following applications and the subsequent elaboration through the book. Nevertheless, having it even schematically in mind at first will illuminate what follows, while the scheme will itself get illuminated by the application in a reciprocal clarification.

**Application
to other
theories**
  A quick reconsideration of the previously outlined theories in the light of this formulation of aesthetic experience will have the advantage of throwing more light on them, and perhaps at the same time will suggest critical refinements on our new one.

We discussed first the position of I. A. Richards in connection with detachment and subjectivism. Richards was forced to his subjectivistic account of the meaning and value of poetry and art in general —in terms of an inner organization of responses and attitudes—by his supposition that *observation*, made systematic in science, is our bedrock rapport with things. This is to suppose that things as *physical objects* are fundamental to everything. Of course, there will be psychological statements, but these too are grounded by observations. The real and the true are thus brought under the hegemony of science. Art will therefore not reveal anything, strictly speaking, but will only organize the subjective responses to a world that is basically physical. I have suggested that this is to mistake a categorial aspect of things—things as physical objects—for things in themselves, and to suppose mistakenly that observation is the only mode of bona fide perception. This is to say that the mistake is in overlooking a categorial option at the base of experience —the phenomenon of categorial aspection. To overlook this is to leave quite unintelligible the persistence or recurrence of nonscientific philosophies. The *anti*-scientific philosophies, by the way, also suffer from categorial-aspect blindness.

Santayana and Bullough, with their notion that aesthetic experience involves an apparent objectification of essentially subjective factors, and the empathists Lipps and Lee, may be critically looked at together. The theme of their philosophy of aesthetic perception is that it is the occasion for a curious sort of appearance. Lee makes it clearest that it is a *mere* appearance. What happens in the aesthetic response is that something that is really on the side of the response—pleasure or kinaesthetic tensions, for example—seems to qualify its object. I say "seems" to make the proposition safe. What is wanting here is the notion of an objective characteristic that perceptibly animates—not qualifies— the thing, an aspect of the thing that is there in aesthetic space for perception in the mode of prehension. Again it is the fact that such characteristics cannot be *observed*, together with the belief that observation is the only mode of objective perception, that is responsible for the tendency of these theorists to leave one with the feeling that aesthetic experience involves an illusion, though a lovely or useful one. (The arguments of Rudolf Arnheim [14] are a good antidote for this common mistake, though they are somewhat spoiled by overstatement.)

The concepts of psychical distance or detachment—the latter term also taking care of Ortega y Gasset's theory—can be given a nice new formulation in terms of aspection and the distinction between the two modes of perception. In these terms, to put oneself at a psychic distance from anything is simply to prehend it. This puts the percipient at a remove from the thing as an object of observation, or as a "physical object," and gets him out of the familiar nonspecial rapport with things of casual perception, if that is where he was before the aesthetic experience. Thus the distance or detachment is not from the thing, on which aesthetic attention bears; rather, the percipient distances himself only from the thing as physical object. By prehending the thing, he actually gets into a special sort of intimacy with it in as much as its aspects are then revealed to him. It is then the thing as aesthetic object, animated by aspects instead of qualified by observable characteristics. Perhaps this is what Ortega y Gasset obliquely had in mind when he spoke of the "psychic flora" that come into view in the aesthetic rapport with things—detached characteristics that observation and everyday perception are blind to.

Another feature of psychical distance is illuminated by our notion of aspects as objective impressions. These characteristics of the thing as aesthetic object are not observed qualities. They appear, rather, in the impressionistic way of looking we have called prehension, and may properly be thought of as the percipient's impressions. But in the aesthetic way of looking they animate the object. They may be found in it. They are not a proper part of the subjective life of the prehender. Thus they may be said to be psychically distanced whereas the free impressions of casual perception and day-dreams had in the usual private way are part of the person having them. In principle, other percipients can therefore share such objective impressions, and the work of art is a special occasion for this. However, the logic of the phrase "having the same impressions" is subtle, to the clarification of which we shall turn at the proper place. What we shall need to provide for is the locution "having the same experience of the thing," where

[14] Rudolf Arnheim, *Art and Visual Perception* (Berkeley: University of California Press, 1954).

the thing is an aesthetic object animated by aspects; that is, where the objectivity of the experience is not to be neglected.

The illusion of art also gets clarified in our new terms. This concept is featured wherever there is the tendency to think of the objectivity of aesthetic experience as involving a projection of subjective states or conditions. This gives one the picture of inner tensions or activities, inner impressions, sensations, or feelings of mass, movement, sound, and color being made to *seem* to qualify the object, by an externalizing act of the imagination. Something gets read into something, without any real displacement of the inner into the outer. The result is thus naturally conceived as illusory, no matter how beautiful and satisfying it is. Illusion, in this picture of it, is necessary to the experiencing of anything as an aesthetic object, especially where the thing is a work of art.

Gombrich's treatment of it is subtle, as we have seen; so is any account with a leaning toward Kantian phenomenalism. (According to this philosophy, things-in-themselves are never experienced, not even as the familiar things of holophrastic perception; only certain constructions of the mind are. So all objects of experience are, in a diffuse, innocuous sense, illusory.) But Gombrich uses the notion of projection in a way more scientific and psychological than it is Kantian, and this forces him to make more of illusion than a wise follower of Kant would. The result for Gombrich is a shifting and perplexing idea of illusion: "Illusion, we will find, is hard to describe or analyze, for though we may be intellectually aware of the fact that any given experience *must* be an illusion, we cannot, strictly speaking, watch ourselves having an illusion" (op. cit., p. 5). Kenneth Clark also speaks of the elusiveness of the illusions that, one way or another, permeate experiences. They are hard to pin down.

This concept of illusion is ambivalent and pervasive because of its failure to discriminate between two modes of perception, each of which has its own standard of objectivity and its own sort of rapport with things that accommodate both, as we have seen. Moreover, the failure to recognize the perceptual mode "seeing as" generates the tantalizing impression that to see anything this way is to inflate it with an illusion. Under this influence Gombrich proceeds to explain such recent trends in art as cubism, formalism, and emphasis on textures as a deliberate attempt to exclude this mode of perception, with its deceptiveness; as if to have a content is to be a deceptive work of art. This does a subtle violence to much art, though it is true that recent art aims at the special effects noticed by Gombrich, effects that will get our attention at the right time.

Dewey's theory of aesthetic experience, which contrasts with the above emphases on detachment and illusion, has the advantage of keeping aesthetic experience where, in some sense, it certainly seems to be, *in medias res*. One does not seem to get away from things, or necessarily to have illusions about them, in aesthetic perception of them. But Dewey's pragmatic theory suffers from the disadvantage of not being discriminating enough on another count—the shift out of one special mode of perception into another. Dewey's account makes it look as if an aesthetic experience is just a consummation or a completion of an observational or a work-a-day experience, and this seems not to be the case. There must be a break of some sort with the ordinary. An account of the break has been given in our new formulation, which shows what sort of connection with things is maintained despite the break with observation of things.

Practically nothing has been made so far of works of art as such. The account has been quite general, with a view to the concept of aesthetic experience. It is interesting to notice that the idea of special ways of looking, no one of which is the model or the starting point for the rest, has become prominent among philosophers of language and experience in the last quarter of a century, under the influence of Wittgenstein's thought in the latter part of his career. This idea has given philosophy a new and promising orientation in epistemology and metaphysics, in their bearings not only on art, but also on religion and science. It is this notion that is exploited here, with some detailing. But we have only broken ground. We must now proceed to examine the concept of a work of art, the consideration of which will, in retrospect, throw more light on aesthetic experience while clarifying the import of our key categories in some other applications.

A WORK OF ART

2

**What
fundamentally
is a work
of art?**
By now you are probably anxious to see specimens of art and
to talk about them more specifically. I, too, will be happier engaged in that sort of discussion, but I must postpone it for the
next chapter, where I shall consider the various arts separately.

In this chapter the categories of art and their related key concepts are to continue to hold our attention as the subject of a general
philosophical discussion of the work of art. Some specific works will
be mentioned incidentally here, but no philosophical examination of
examples from the arts can be very penetrating until the concepts of
materials, medium, form, content, subject matter, expression, and representation have been illuminated by general considerations. Only through
such illumination can they become effective instruments of exposition,
analysis, and criticism of particular art works.

The phrase "work of art" is in philosophical aesthetics rather
like "meaning" in the philosophy of language. It is vague because it
serves some sort of core or basic purpose; this makes its use overlap
with that of other more special terms both in common parlance and
in the language of the specialists. This has induced some theorists to
suggest getting along without these vague terms. But where this has
been attempted, some surrogate expression has usually been brought in
by the back door to do the same multidimensional job of the banished
one. The reason for this is that the usefulness of the term "work of art"
is owing to this very ambivalence. But some pinning down of the way
it is to be used here—even if it is not always so used by everybody—
will be helpful if the restriction does not violate the basic or root use
it commonly has, and if it rules out of order certain peripheral or

28

occasional uses that amount to abuses, trouble-breeders for the theory of art. Let us see next what some of these abuses are, and what is wrong with them.

What fundamentally is a work of art? Answers have been suggested by the treatment of aesthetic experience in Chapter 1, but it is time to examine this question not so much by differentiating modes of perception as by focusing on the work of art itself as the object of perception. Generally speaking, there are four sorts of answers to the question, none of which quite satisfies our curiosity. Consideration of these answers will show that they gravitate around the notions of the materials and the media of art, which will be discussed after this exposition of the four off-beat answers to the question, and of one that we hope is right.

The philosopher of art who is an idealist or spiritualist in his metaphysics categorically denies that the work of art is physical. In fact, nothing is fundamentally physical according to his theory. Even what we call physical nature in space and time is how Spirit or Mind looks when it has externalized or objectified itself to the limit of otherness from itself. Thus even physical objects are the inert products of a mental operation; they are themselves of the stuff of mind, but deployed in a mechanical and abstract fashion that misrepresents their essential nature. So even the physical world, although not strictly a work of art, is a work of mind.

Since the physical sciences investigate this lifeless appearance of a spiritual reality by dissociating it from its true source, art is said by the idealists to be more revealing of the nature of things than is science. Art more clearly reveals that both the productive operations and the finished products are mental or spiritual. In fact, artistic vision of nature itself will disclose nature's fundamental spirituality, presenting it so clearly as a work of mind that it registers as a work of cosmic art. This notion is celebrated in the works of the great romantic artists. Wordsworth, Goethe, Beethoven, and Wagner are good examples. The key concept of this philosophy of art is imagination, and this suggests that a creative spiritual activity orders reality in ways too subtle for objective, scientific reason to grasp.

But a work of art in the more special sense is, in this view, an inner creation of the imagination, to be distinguished from the external embodiment in a physical medium or material. This is to keep it as uncontaminated as possible by matter or the inanimate abstractions that hoodwink the scientists—what F. H. Bradley called the "ballet of bloodless categories." Also, it makes it possible in principle for one to be an artist without working with the materials of art; that is, without embodying or materializing the art object. The true creative work is the inner intuition and formulation of the work of art as emotionally charged image. Embodying this in an external material, if it occurs at all, is an affair of technical skill, not an essential part either of the creative act of inner expression or of the finished work of art resplendent in the inner light of the creator-mind. Such a conception, allowing for the possibility of many mute and unsung Miltons in art, is developed by Benedetto Croce.[1] A much friendlier—and saner—view of the objective materials and media of art is taken by another neo-idealist in metaphysics, Bernard Bosanquet,[2] who stresses the transforming power of the medium under the reciprocally transforming work on it of the artist's subjective demands. The work of art is thus a function of these two factors, both appearing, however, as sustained in Objective Mind—the ultimate reality in the final metaphysical picture.

The second answer to our question agrees and disagrees with the first. The work of art is not physical. But neither is it mental. It is a *tertium quid*, a third sort of somewhat, like a Platonic universal. This is the position of logical realism. Its model is the timeless and placeless logical universal of thought or conception, such as triangularity or redness. By analogy with these, the universality, even timelessness, of a great work of art is thought to be explained. And as one sees the logical universal with the eye of intellect, so one beholds the work of art with the eye of educated imagination which, in aesthetic contemplation, is rather like intellect suffused with emotion. According to this view, what the artist does is not so much to create the art object but to reveal it, via the medium, to the organ of aesthetic vision. What is literally constructed is the arrangement of elements of the medium, which then becomes the occasion for selective contemplation of an eternal form among an infinity of other possible ones. The essentially invisible is thus made visible. This particularization is sometimes thought of in a Platonic vein as a necessary degradation of something in itself perfect. Heard (embodied) melodies are sweet but those unheard are sweeter, said Keats. But such limitation of the universal by presenting it to sense and imagination is a necessary function of the artist. There is a tendency among these logical realists to let the notion of the work of art as the materialized universal replace the notion of the work of art as the universal *per se*. This tends to make the materials and the medium of the art more relevant to the work of the artist as artist. Some passages in George Santayana's *Scepticism and Animal Faith*[3] present such a logical-realistic conception of a work of art, though in a more naturalistic setting than that of the Platonists.

---

[1] Benedetto Croce, "Intuition and Expression," *A Modern Book of Esthetics*, ed. Melvin Rader (New York: Holt, Rinehart & Winston, Inc., 1960), pp. 88–101.

[2] *Three Lectures on Aesthetic* (London: Macmillan and Co., Ltd., 1915), pp. 222–27.

[3] *Scepticism and Animal Faith* (New York: Charles Scribner's Sons, 1923).

The phenomenalist's answer to the question agrees with the notion that a work of art is not physical, while rejecting the Platonic conception of it as a universal entity. A work of art is a class of appearances satisfying certain requirements of coherence and comprehensiveness. Thus it is not just any perceptual object, but a perceptual object of a certain kind, an aesthetic object. This, strictly speaking, is the work of art, or what the artist creates and exhibits in the medium of the art. The phenomenalist will occasionally notice this connection of the work of art with its physical basis. But, he argues, since the physical as such is not strictly given in perception, it must not be thought of as a proper part of the work of art. However, the ambiguity of "work of art" makes some phenomenalists hesitate about this. After all, people do naturally say that works of art hang on museum walls and are transported in moving vans; this is to recognize them as physical objects. To escape this difficulty for his denial that they are physical, the phenomenalist proposes that "work of art" be equated with "aesthetic object," which is not what one hangs on the wall, strictly speaking. I have in mind such a theory as that of Beardsley.

The presupposition of a pure phenomenalism is that physical objects are themselves constructions out of sensory appearances. But "impure" phenomenalism holds that physical objects and events are the external, imperceptible conditions of the appearances, in some sense causing their appearances. It is this notion that affiliates Beardsley's theory with epiphenomenalism, a metaphysics that requires everything to be fundamentally physical. This embarrasses the notion of any other kind of object such as the aesthetic. Beardsley notices this in his treatment of works of art, and wonders whether they should be called objects at all. "Aesthetic objects . . . are . . . objects *manqués*. There is something lacking in them that keeps them from being quite real, from achieving the full status of things."

The fourth type of answer makes a sophisticated linguistic point concerning what a work of art is fundamentally. Yes, the work of art is basically physical, but there are two ways of talking about it. "Work of art" has two different uses in reference to the same thing. We are to think of this thing, the work of art, as physical, but we must be careful to recognize an aesthetic use of the expression "work of art" and its cognates. For example, Margaret Macdonald [4] says that works of plastic art are physical objects like any stone or star. Performances of literary and musical works of art, whose common medium is sound, are physical events. The distinction between these physical works of art and their manifestations is not a distinction between two kinds of objects. The way out of the puzzles of dualistic theories, she suggests, is to recognize that there are two uses of the key terms in talk about art, and that

[4] "Art and Imagination," *Proc. Arist. Soc.*, LIII (1953), 205–26.

this does not imply that there are two kinds of objects corresponding to the uses. A similar position is argued by Paul Ziff,[5] who is concerned with annihiliating "that ghost of aesthetics, the mysterious aesthetic object."

An answer suggested

What is wrong, and what is right, with these answers to our question? Let us attempt to find out by considering another question which is going to look queer at first. What is missing in the accounts above is, I believe, the previously mentioned concept of "material thing" and its categorial aspects—its manifestation as a physical or as an aesthetic object. The queer question, posed to throw light on what the theorists above have obliquely in view, is: where is a work of art? This question seems strange because ordinarily it is asked with a particular work in mind: is "Guernica" in the Guggenheim Museum or the Museum of Modern Art? But my question is not only a more general one, but a curious kind that recent Anglo-American philosophy warns us against. Nevertheless, I am going to ask several such questions, though I shall try to answer them with the care and caution that the new concern with language has encouraged with fine passion. My question is rather like the one I might ask myself as a philosopher: where is my friend? while I look at him beside me in the chair in my study. The answer, in the chair there beside me, will not do at all. That by-passes the sense of my question. I have a philosophical problem buzzing around in me, like the fly in the bottle trying to get out. In my friend's face, and in the lips pursed around his pipe, I notice his thoughtfulness and his sympathetic concern to assist me in my own thinking about the question. These mental characteristics are included in the person of whose presence I am aware. Of this person I ask, where is he? as I look at him. Shall I say that his mental activity is in his body and his body is in the chair, therefore his mind or the thoughtful part of it is in the chair? Remember, I am asking where the *person* is, not just his body. And it is this problem that may be generalized in the question, where is a person, any person? Couched this way, it reveals itself as connected with questions about spaces and how things are or are not located in them. P. F. Strawson[6] suggests that "person" has an Ur- (root or basic) sense, presupposed by the sophisticated distinction between body and animating mind. The question about the location of a person is therefore of a different logical type from the same question about the body and the mind separately.

[5] Paul Ziff, "Art and the 'Object of Art'," *Mind*, LX (October 1951), 466–80; selection in Elton, *Aesthetics and Language* (New York: Philosophical Library, 1954).

[6] *Individuals* (London: Methuen & Co. Ltd., 1959).

The question "Where is a work of art?" turns out to be problematic for similar reasons. Here, too, we have a material something animated by something, though this time by an emotionally charged image, not by a mind, as in the case of a person. This leaves us with a similar ambivalence of the term "work of art." It too, simply as a material thing, has an Ur-meaning presupposed by the distinction between the work as a physical object and as an aesthetic object involving its categorial aspects. Therefore questions about its location will be of three different logical types, "space" and "place" having a different meaning in each case, with corresponding variations in the sense of "perceive."

1. Suppose it is a painting—Van Gogh's "The Yellow Chair" since we were speaking of chairs. We have seen what locating it as a physical object means, and how this involves accepting what it is related to in physical space—the wall and other things in the room—as physical objects also. What animates the picture, the chair image charged with the feeling of comfortable domesticity, is not anywhere at all in this physical space—as a person's mind is not in the space of his body as an observed physical object.

2. Locating it as an aesthetic object, we focus on the medium of the picture's materials, in which the image forms while taking on properties of aesthetic space. Asking where the picture is in this sense is, in effect, asking where *what it is prehended as* is, or where the elements of this prehension are in the space of the picture, a question quite different from the first. We shall discuss this further later on.

3. But people do make sense of and answer questions about the location of a work of art, just as they do of a person, simply as such or without the sophisticated categorial controls of the first two questions. "In his study," they say, or "It's over there in the Metropolitan Museum," meaning to locate thereby the person as such or the work of art as such. This is to use the terms in their Ur-senses, and is characteristic of plain talk. In such cases, "there," "place," and "space" have a similar use, indicating the familiar, nonspecial milieu of holophrastic perception, where things are "simply" located, encountered, and talked about.

What these general considerations are intended to achieve is to place the concept of the work of art in a light that explains and even justifies—instead of embarrassing—the useful ambivalence it actually has in our talk about works of art. Moreover, they are intended to drive home the fact of the ambivalent nature of a work of art, which accounts for the perplexing possibility of looking at it in one way while the logical framework of a given consideration presupposes another. In such cases, the perceptual grounds for sense-making of a certain type will be overlooked, resulting in conceptual confusion. It is as important to explore these as to iron out the logic of the language appropriate to the given mode of perception.

Application
to other
theories So let us now apply all this, in the spirit of moderators, to the four views of a work of art that we examined before. This can be done briefly, in the form of critical suggestions.

The idealistic view, which holds that the work of art is a mental or spiritual thing, is wrong so far. It is right in supposing that the work of art as an aesthetic object is dissociated from the physical. The mistake of idealism consists in supposing that because it is not physical, it is disconnected from the material thing. This tempts one on to the conclusion that it is simply subjective and therefore mental —a curious sort of subjective object. The idealist of the Crocean variety reaches this distorted position because he is operating only with the upper half of our diagram (p. 23). Thus, supposing that the only aspect of material things is physical, and realizing that the physical aspect is not relevant to the work of art as an object of aesthetic perception, he has to back up into the subjective and the mental to find a place for the aesthetic object. He has overlooked a whole mode of perception of things—prehension—in which they, the material things, are presented as aesthetic objects with their own sort of objectivity (the lower part of the diagram). This is the shape of Croce's mistake. Bosanquet, distrusting such subjectivism as a "false idealism," attempts to give a true one by picturing the subjective and the objective factors (still on the upper half of the diagram only) in a mutual interpenetration which puts some soul into the physical while giving this animating principle or mind a body. A work of art, according to Bosanquet, best exhibits this amalgamation.

The answer of Platonic (logical) realism also stems from the awareness that the work of art, in its relevance to aesthetic experience, is not a physical object. But this view has, in addition, the merit of refusing to subjectify or mentalize it. Its mistake consists in supposing that, since the work of art is not in the space and time of physical objects, it is a spaceless and timeless entity like a logical universal. This is to overlook the aesthetic space and time in which *things* appear as aesthetic objects, a milieu in which they have a history, unlike eternal universals, but a history not like that of physical particulars.

The phenomenalist who contends that physical objects are the basis of the more tenuous objects of aesthetic perception is at a loss over what to make of the latter, since he also, like the other theorists, denies that they are physical.[7] How then is one to account for the full-

[7] Monroe Beardsley, *Aesthetics* (New York: Harcourt, Brace & World, Inc., 1958), pp. 54–55.

bodied and whole-souled thing called a work of art, if this, as an aesthetic object, is identified simply with a set of appearances? To satisfy this demand for thinghood, the phenomenalist posits the aesthetic object as not identical with any one or any subset of its perceptual presentations. It is, rather, the whole set or class of them. But this still does not provide for its being any *thing*—the thing that is presented on this or that occasion. And the phenomenalist cannot make this provision because he has only the concepts of the physical object and of appearance to work with, which are basic in his system; they are his primitives. What he lacks is the notion of a material thing—the work of art—appearing as an aesthetic object. (Physical objects never appear as aesthetic objects; to say they do is to commit what philosophers now call a "category-mistake.")

The answer of the philosopher of language is cagey, and correct in its reflection on the multiple uses of expressions in talk about art. But if one leaves untouched the presumption that it is the physical object that is there as the underlying referent both of the talk about art and of the aesthetic experience, at least in the case of the plastic arts, then the temptation to turn idealist or Platonist or phenomenalist in the philosophy of art will be left standing, and the linguistic dualism itself will be left unexplained. Along with the notion of an aesthetic use of terms must go the notion of the corresponding way of looking at the things being thus articulated. One who overlooks this is simply ignoring the fact that it is *things*, in a certain perception of them—Sibley called it an appropriate sort of noticing—that demand the aesthetic use of terms in the language of art. To try to make the linguistic distinction alone do the job, in the presence of allegedly basic physical objects, is to invite miscarriages in thinking about the issue.

Here ends the general discussion of the concept of a work of art. There are important facets of the concept—medium, form, and content, for example—yet to be considered, and without this consideration the general concept is left pretty empty. We shall turn now to examining each of these facets specifically.

Materials and medium   The previous treatment of "material thing" in connection with "work of art" generates correlated questions about the concepts of the materials and the medium of a work of art. Here we shall give an analysis of the concepts as applicable to any work of art. The account of the materials and media of the various arts, taken one at a time, will occupy us in the third chapter. There we shall notice significant differences as we pass from one art to another.

I took care not to say, "materials *or* medium," because the concepts are distinct, not synonymous. Where one strictly applies, the other does not. The failure to notice the difference has spawned confusions that have occasionally had unfortunate effects even on the first principles of the theory of art.

To aid in our discussion of the materials of art, let us make a verbal map of the ground to be covered in the rest of this chapter:

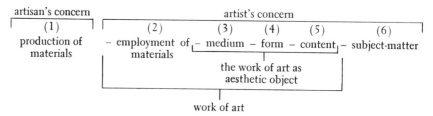

Let us think of this chart as representing the field of art in the widest sense, where the artists, along with artisans who produce art goods for them, form a sort of colony in which the activities relevant to art are carried on and where the finished compositions are located.

Our first question concerns the materials of art. In the attempt to answer this question one may, as a philosopher, probe too far down to strata that have no special relevance to art. For example, matter as such, or in some general sense, is not among the materials of art. Nor is petrified matter (stone), colored matter, or noisy events, as such. One gets to the fundamental materials of art when one gets to its "instruments," in the straightforward, popular sense of the word, as in musical instruments: violins, pianos, flutes, clarinets. These are produced or made. So are brushes and pigments and pastels and canvasses. So are units of quarried stone and masses of bronze. All these are art materials as instruments. They are the solid productions of "artists" in the old Greek sense of makers of material goods. Let us call those makers "artisans." They produce what "artists" in the other (relevant) sense go to art goods stores to buy. The materials of the arts, in the bedrock, subaesthetic sense of "matter" that has any relevance to art, are thus these things that serve the artists as instruments. As a musician plays on strings or a woodwind, so the painter plays on pigments, where all these materials have been produced for him by artisans of the arts. (Literature seems to lack "materials" in the sense of instruments produced by artisans; we shall see later if this is so.)

Though the same person may be proficient both as an artisan of the art—he may make his own pigments excellently by a secret formula for durability, for example—and as an artist, the two functions are quite distinct. There is no necessary connection between them. An artist may be great without being also an artisan of the art. One does not have to be a Stradivarius in order to be a Heifetz. This fact should be kept in mind by sentimental philosophers of the relation between art and scientific technology, who tend to describe artists and artisans in practically the same language. What tempts them to make this friendly mistake is the fact that a good artisan—a Stradivarius—will construct a violin with an educated ear for the quality of the tone. But his skill and his wisdom bear on the wood, the aging, the gut, the glue, the varnish (an important item for tone quality). These are the artisan's instruments, the materials with which he composes the violin. But the finished violin is the *artist's* instrument. The violin and the bow are his materials. With these, he produces or performs the musical work of art, or has them in view if he is composing for the violin.

The difference may be put in terms of our previous concepts of "material thing" and "physical object." The maker of the materials of the art, the artisan, will have more occasion to look on the finished instrument as a physical object, since he operates with the elements that enter into its composition. He must have the know-how and the know-what of the "analysis" of the finished product that is the artist's instrument. But the artist, in principle, need never experience his instrument as a physical object, only as a material thing. The artist gets the feel of his instrument as he composes with it—the feel of the brush, the feel of the keyboard. But one does not get the feel of anything as a physical object. What we mean by "physical object" is a material thing presented in a field of perception (observation) from which feelings, including sensory "impressions," have been excluded as irrelevant. So the remark that one does not get the feel of anything as a physical object is a part of philosophical grammar, a logical and phenomenological grammar. A material thing is, however, a large enough potential to accommodate feelings. Such accommodation may be described either as the thing's incorporating the feelings, or its being incorporated by them; the latter description may be given by the artist who experiences the instrument "becoming a part of himself." This must not be mistaken as saying that the instrument—pigment, string, English horn—as a material thing becomes an ingredient in the aesthetics of the work of art, and thus a proper part of the artist's composition. Later consideration of this delicate point will confirm that the artist's feel of the instrument is, rather, a condition of his successfully employing it, not as such a part of his composition or work of art. (We shall see, however, that even this can be made the subject matter and the content of the work of art, though it usually is not.)

We are on the threshold of the concept of the medium here, but before crossing it, let us notice something more about tone from the point of view of the instrument maker, the artisan. He is very much concerned about tone. In fact, his composition, the finished instrument, is successful only if its tone is right. "Tone" here is quite naturally stretched to apply to the quality of a note, a color, a piece of quarried marble. The tone will have a certain timbre, and this is everything. A note sounded on a cello does not have the timbre it would have if sounded on a harp, violin, piano, or harpsichord—though all these instruments are stringed. This holds for pigments. The sensitive eye will visually feel the differences in the timbres of different pigments of the same color. A little change in the lighting will make this difference in the timbre more appreciable to the uneducated eye.

As you distinguish one person from another in the dark by the timbre of the voice, even if each sounds only the same single note, so you may distinguish the various instruments of different kinds and different instruments of the same kind—Segovia's Spanish guitar from the one you buy at Macy's for ten dollars. Such remarks tempt one on to stretch the notion of "timbre" to suggest that the timbre of the tone expresses the character of the whole instrument, or is its soul, in which the material instrument comes to life for the aesthetic purposes of the artist employing it. One hears or sees the whole instrument when he experiences the timbre. As a man sees character in a human face, the expert perceives the character of the instrument in the timbre of its tone. Thus he sees not just the color tone but also the character of the *pigment* in it; he listens to the *violin* whose character he gets in its tonal quality. You will not understand the great artisan's or the great artist's love of the instrument if you overlook this. Nor will you understand how the work of art proper is grounded in the nature of the *things* that are its materials. (Put "physical objects" in place of "things" in that statement, and you get a real howler. "Howler" here is a bad logical mistake, a confusion of categories.)

This animation of the (primary) material of the art is not the work of the artist. The tribute for it goes to the artisan. The artist simply accepts it and works with it as the medium, not the material, of his art.

A final distinction about materials is necessary here. I spoke above of brush and pigment, and of bow and violin, in the same breath, as if each of these instruments of the painter or the violinist were his materials in the same sense. Clearly they are not. Only the pigment has timbre in its color. Certainly the brush has none. The brush is used to apply and arrange the pigment. The painter operates with the brush in the employment of the pigment, but the latter is closer to his aesthetic purpose and is therefore his "primary" instrument. The brush is, then, a "secondary" instrument. Now we can be more precise about what it is that the artist gets the feel of in the manipulation of materials. He gets the feel strictly of the brush, not of the pigment, whose feel is the color timbre fixed by the pigment's character. He simply sees this. Similarly, the sounded strings of a piano (the timbre of whose notes expresses the character of the whole instrument) are the primary material or instrument of the pianist as artist. The keyboard and its connections with the hammers for sounding the strings are the secondary instruments. The good pianist will, by practice, get the feel of the keyboard, not of the strings whose timbre he simply hears. And the chisels of the sculptor stand to the stone with its timbre as a keyboard stands to strings, as a brush stands to pigment, and as a camera stands to the developed film. It is of such secondary instruments that the artist gets the feel by manipulation. In general, one may say that the artist works *on* the primary materials of his art *with* the secondary.

In most philosophies of art, it is instructive to notice how inadequate is the notice taken of the materials of art, if we take "materials" to mean instruments as described above. The reason for this is that materials are commonly thought of as just physical objects, strictly beneath the notice of the artist. This is to overlook how integral they are as *material things* to his enterprise. They are its material, if not physical, basis, and the artist works lovingly with them and on them, as, on categorial principle, he cannot do with physical objects.

Now that we have examined the primary and secondary materials of art as its instruments, we are ready to discuss the medium. In view of the foregoing treatment of materials, the consideration of medium can be quite brief.

Even the primary materials (instruments) of the arts are still not their media. The string or the pigment or the stone, even after being prepared by the artisan for use by the artist, is not the medium of the art. Moreover, it is not the medium even while the artist is using it, or in the final pattern he gives it in the accomplished work of art. In this final state, the primary materials of the art have been manipulated by the artist into a material thing—the work of art—specially designed to be prehended as an aesthetic object. Of course, in the process of composition, the materials themselves are material things for the artist, not physical objects. He does not observe them. Rather, he prehends the timbre of the tone of each material element—color, sound, texture—then orchestrates the materials for the sake of the composite tonality of their combined tones. This is the formulated medium of the work of art, in which the artist presents, for prehension, the content of the work. (Content is discussed later.) Strictly speaking, the artist does not manipulate the medium. He composes with it, or with the tonal timbres of the elements of his primary materials, and these tonal characteristics are his medium in the basic sense. He composes with these in view until he gets the pattern of them that captures what he wants exhibited (content) to prehensive vision. He composes *with*, he does not work *on* the timbres. He composes with the timbres of his materials by *working on* the *materials*. The former are his medium, and they, not the materials, are proper elementary parts of the work of art as an aesthetic object. The materials are parts of the work of art simply as a material thing. But one should never forget that it is these materials, arranged by the artist into the material thing called the work of art, that are prehended as the aesthetic object. In the artist's experience as he composes, each material is featured as a little, elementary aesthetic object. Thus the composite aesthetic object is not a sort of ethereal veil or screen between the prehending subject and the work of art. The aesthetic object *is* the ordered material thing (work of art) appearing under the categorial aspect that *it* has for prehensive perception. This remark is made to lay the ghost of "the aesthetic object" [8] as wrongly conceived. In short, the medium of a material thing is what is featured in prehension of the thing as aesthetic object. And in observation the medium is excluded, because the thing is then a physical object.

The philosophical literature on materials and media is extensive, but on the whole it suffers from insufficient attention to the materials of art as its instruments in the music store or the art supply store sense of the term. This usually results in an unsatisfactory distinction between the material and the medium of the art, and leaves the philosopher of art unable to explain what has gone on in art, especially in the first half of the twentieth century. More on this later. T. M. Greene [9] gives a solid, traditional kind of coverage, although his use of "primary" and "secondary" materials differs from our use. Maurice Grosser [10] offers a fresh account of the materials and the medium of painting, helping one to develop important insights. Most helpful is D. W. Prall's treatment of aesthetic orders. [11]

Form, content, and subject matter   In discussing the medium we were beginning to move within the ambit of the work of art as an aesthetic object. We get still nearer the heart of this affair as we proceed to the form and the content of the work of art. For convenience, I shall from here on speak simply of the work of art, meaning this as an aesthetic object without always saying so. But it should be repeated in this con-

[8] Paul Ziff, *loc. cit.*

[9] *The Arts and The Art of Criticism* (Princeton: Princeton University Press, 1940).

[10] *The Painter's Eye* (New York: Holt, Rinehart & Winston, Inc., 1951); and (New York: New American Library, Mentor edition, MT 371, 1956).

[11] "Sensuous Elements and Esthetic Orders," *A Modern Book of Esthetics*, ed. Melvin Rader (New York: Holt, Rinehart & Winston, Inc., 1960), pp. 227–40.

nection that the work of art is fundamentally a material thing, and this is what is manifested as an aesthetic object. What follows from this fact is a subtle but very important point: that characterizations of works of art—descriptive, interpretive, and critical—are not *fundamentally* about aesthetic objects. For example, it is not the aesthetic object that is, strictly speaking, bright and beautiful. The work of art, the materials patterned in a certain way, may be bright and beautiful as an aesthetic object. The fundamental subject of predication is the work of art, not the aesthetic object. This point will be developed in Chapter 4.

Any account of form and content in art is at a disadvantage if it tries to get along without reference to the subject matter of art, though the latter is indeed extraneous to work of art proper, as the diagram on p. 36 shows. In fact, even the concept of the medium, which is internal to the work, changes complexion as it is related to all these concepts, as we shall see.

So, first let us connect them all in a single statement and then consider them and their relations in separate analyses. One may say that the *content* of a work of art is its *subject matter* as *formulated* in its *medium*. Here we have all four concepts with some indication as to how they are related. There are equivalent statements that present significant options. One could say instead that the *form* and *medium* of a work of art are that by virtue of which the artist transfigures its *subject matter* into its *content*. (In these statements I am deliberately, but with difficulty, refraining from using "represent" and "express" because I want later to illuminate the concepts of representation and expression in the light of the concepts discussed here and in the previous section.)

Consider first, for illustration of the general thesis, not a work of art but just a thing like the bit of driftwood I have on my mantelpiece. It has roughly the shape (form) of a sea lion. By virtue of this form I see it *as* a sea lion. The sea lion that I see the wooden figure as is its content, and it is this objective image that animates the material of the figure. The image as such, without the embodiment, is the subject matter of the piece of driftwood seen as a sea lion. As subject matter, this is simply the image of a sea lion. You can have or get such an image in two ways: (1) by imaging it with your eyes shut, or by looking at a sea lion; (since a percept is also a species of image, having the image in either of these ways is to be aware of subject matter) and (2) with your eyes open, seeing something you know is not a sea lion (the driftwood figure) as one. The image is then the content of the thing prehended as an aesthetic object. This is how the term "content" is to be used. In such cases, you are not simply *imagining* that something *is* something, you are *perceiving* it *as* something.

But what of the medium? And the material? It is quite proper to say that, with this driftwood, the tonalities of the material (medium) count for nothing. Any chunk of stuff with this shape may be seen as a sea lion. Indeed, a pencilled outline on paper, with no portrayal at all of the stuff of the thing, would be seen as a sea lion in the same way. In view of this one might say that this driftwood figure lacks both medium and material. It is the form, as the bare shape of the thing, that carries the image as content. Yet, from another angle, one could say that the material of the figure is animated into a kind of medium in which the image is presented for prehension, thanks mainly to the form. The driftwood is thus beginning to appear in aesthetic space, with a voluminousness and suggested color tonality that it does not have either as a physical object or as just a material thing.

This is the kind of question one runs into when the thing is not a work of art, but it is amenable nevertheless to "aesthetic experience" in some rudimentary sense—a sense so attenuated that the expression was not devised for such applications. It is usually reserved for things that satisfy more, or at least other, conditions. I think first of the natural things not produced by art, and not formed in any significant way even by nature, but having rich color or sound textures and tonalities (thundering sunsets, for example). Perhaps "aesthetic" is more apt in such cases than with the driftwood, where only the shape counts, because of the original meaning of the term *aesthesis*, connecting it with the sensory "feels" of things, their aesthetic surfaces.[12] The sky, a piece of velvet, a running brook are "aesthetic objects" in this manner of speaking, simply with their tonalities in view. To experience things this way is already to be aware of them as aesthetic objects instead of physical objects, though the thing in question is not, at this rudimentary level, being seen as something else, as it would be if the aesthetic object were a cloud with the shape of a man's head. To be attentive to these elementary sensory values is to assume the stance necessary to a more articulate aesthetic experience—including the additional factor of seeing something *as* something—the occasion for which is a work of art. So, we return to works of art, in which medium, content, and form are featured in relation to materials and subject-matter for the sake of a greater aesthetic articulateness than things in the state of nature provide. The materials from one side, the subject matter from the other, are transfigured in the work of art as aesthetic object. Look again at the diagram.

[12] Paul Weiss, *The World of Art* (Carbondale, Ill.: Southern Illinois University Press, 1961).

The artist, having attuned himself to the tonalities (timbres) of his primary materials or instruments, has made the elements of his medium available for composition, as we have seen. The timbres of the tones are the elements of the medium. He composes *with* these, not *on* them. What he works on are his primary materials. One can make and apply a paint, and then wipe it off the canvas, but one cannot make, apply, and then wipe off a color tone. (This is a grammatical or logical remark about concepts, not a statement of impotence.) As he works on his instrument, the artist has several things in view: (1) a certain form or pattern of the elements of the medium; (2) an image of something, usually suffused by an emotion (sometimes only the image, sometimes only the emotion) to be featured in the work of art, its subject matter; and (3) the content of the work that takes shape in the medium as the latter is formulated (patterned) by the manipulation of the instruments or materials of the art. This complex manipulation is controlled by a comprehensive view of all these factors at once, working towards a composition that will exhibit the subject matter as its content.

A quick example: "The Two Lovers," by Modigliani. The title refers to the subject matter which, even without looking at the picture, one gets, in a general way, including the associated ideas, images, and feelings. The two lovers one sees in the picture are its content. Now one is seeing something as something, in the aesthetic space of the picture. This is not a case of *imagining* that something is something, as a child imagines that its doll is a baby and acts accordingly; it would be hopelessly inept to ask someone to imagine that the two figures in the painting are lovers, although if the composition were even more abstract, it might help to ask him to *see* them *as* two lovers. (This, in effect, is the aesthetically relevant function of titles of works of art.) Modigliani has composed the elements of the medium—tonalities of pigment on canvas—into a pattern that is the form. He has formulated the medium by working on the materials until the composition may be seen as two lovers in picture space. The *style* of the composition forces attention away from the subject matter as such to both the content and the medium. The latter is the very substance of the work of art as an aesthetic object.

Let us now take a closer look at form and content in a work of art, in relation to subject matter outside it.

The form of a work of art is the arrangement or pattern of the elements (tonal values) of its medium, not simply of its materials. An aesthetically insensitive or blind person may notice (observe) the arrangement of the materials in physical space—notes, colors, contours—without noticing their relationships as aesthetic elements of the *medium* of the art. That is, he will be blind to their relationships as tonal values in aesthetic space, or to what they do to one another in such relations. This is to overlook the first-order form of the work of art as an aesthetic object. In short, he will be unaware of the data that have any aesthetic relevance to descriptions, interpretations, and evaluations of the composition, and not prehending these, he will certainly not get their arrangement or form, their pattern. Since the aesthetic space of the composition is structured by the way the elements of the medium are related, and since these relations or intervals are determined in part by such characteristics as smoothness, harshness, warmth, sharpness, or delicacy of sounds, colors, or lines, blindness to the elements of the medium causes blindness to how they are related in the space of the composition, or to its form. For example, a gray-bluish green is intrinsically farther back in the space of the picture than is a bright tan, though the artist may compose the elements in a manner that forces the green closer to the picture's plane (foreground), thus producing a dynamic tension. If one cannot prehend this sort of phenomena, for him there is no ground for aesthetic considerations of any kind.

The form, or the arrangement of the medium's elements in the aesthetic space of the composition, is not determined only by their intrinsic values. Their relationships are modified also by the content of the composition, which is what it is seen as, or by the subject matter realized in the medium. Thus a bright motif may by itself tend to protrude, but seen as a sunlit wheat field in the background of the composition, it will tend to be recessed. (Gauguin provides good examples of this.) The interplay of these forces will determine the position of the medium's element in the aesthetic space of the work of art. This is its "second-order" form. Similar remarks hold for a musical phrase that may be intimate by its intrinsic brilliance but distanced into a background motif as an element in the aesthetic volume of a pensive composition.

For the formalists in philosophical aesthetics, form is everything. It is of the essence of the work of art. Their primary concern is that perception or experience be diverted in art from its subject matter to its content on the one hand, and from its bare materials or material basis to its medium and form on the other. They are not wrong about that. What has induced them into an overstatement in favor of form is their inadequate conception of the content animating the medium (not material), when the medium takes on the right form in a good composition. Also to blame for their overemphasis of form is their failure to distinguish content from subject matter. Some of the contentions of the formalists, such as Clive Bell, Roger Fry, and Hanslick, will be assessed in chapters 3 and 4.

The content of a work of art is the subject matter of the work realized (formulated) in its medium, for perception in the mode of prehension. There is a standing controversy about the relationship of subject matter, which is external to the work, to the form or the elements of the design, and to the content. In a recent debate, the question of whether there is ever a real fusion was discussd by George Dickie and Monroe Beardsley.[13] Examining this debate will throw some more light on these key concepts. Here let me say merely that both thinkers—Dickie more than Beardsley—try to get along with only one notion of space. This tends to make pure design with its plastic elements into data for observation. In this vein, they are mere geometric shapes in a Euclidean pattern. How then can they, strictly speaking, fuse with an emotion (cheerfulness of a smile) or even an image as subject matter? They probably cannot fuse with an emotion, Dickie answers; they can fuse with an image only in the sense of having shapes observably similar to such space properties, including bulkiness, of the originals (subject matter). This makes aesthetic perception into an implicit confused *observation* of resemblances between the work of art and the original subject matter. Beardsley, in reply, wisely points to the phenomenon of depth in works of art (third dimension) without which fundamental condition there is no aesthetic experience at all. But he does not make enough of this. He fails to make it clear that a shape or design as observed is not what it is as prehended in the aesthetic space of the composition. In that milieu, the shape is not the outline of a flat patch of pigment on canvas; it is the form of an (objective) image, prehended in the medium and functioning as a part of the content of the work; the shape, for example, of a bent back or a drooping fold of a garment, as in Giotto's "Lamentations Over Christ" (the debaters' own example). That sadness fuses with this is perhaps even less problematic than how it fuses with the shape of the bent back of one's bereaved neighbor. In both cases, something is obviously animated with an emotion; the medium and content of the composition in one case, the neighbor in the other. Perplexity arises in the aesthetic case only if one supposes that the work of art is basically a physical object having only that sort of space properties. Replace "physical object" with "material thing" especially designed for prehension as an aesthetic object in a space that is the native habitat of images and emotions; keep in mind how accommodating *any* material thing is to such perception; and then

[13] George Dickie, "Design and Subject Matter," and Monroe Beardsley, "Representation and Presentation: a Reply to Professor Dickie," *Journal of Philosophy*, LVIII (April 27, 1961), 233–38 and 238–41.

the perplexity about fusion is dissipated. Anyway, the fusion then ceases to be a *specially* mysterious phenomenon. The resolution of the difficulty stems from an adequate notion of the content of the work of art as the presentation of the subject matter in the medium for prehensive perception. How can this happen? Well, how can you experience the sadness in your neighbor's face? Or in his voice? Similar perplexities arise even here if you have a sneaking suspicion—as some philosophers have—that, strictly speaking, your perception presents you with nothing but a physical object in motion. The rest, the animation, has to be conjured up, according to them, by subjective associations and analogies. Well, *is* it?

A word about the style of a work of art. Is it a sort of form? The distinction is delicate, but there is one. The style of the work of art is the style of the artist, if he is not imitating. But we do not say that the form of the work is the form of the artist. Form belongs only on the objective side. Style cuts across the subjective-objective distinction.

So I suggest that the style of a work of art is to the whole work what the timbre or tonality of a note is to the whole instrument as used by the artist to produce it. The character (quality) of the instrument in use is revealed in the timbre, as we have seen. Well, the character of the composition is exhibited in its style. This includes the quality of the artist as the composer, but only as a part. Rhetorical overstatements have been made about this, such as the famous dictum that the style is the man ("Le style, c'est l'homme," said Proudhon). Yet, they make a point worth making. After all, the spirit of the artist is the milieu in which he first considers the subject matter, and his special way of prehending it colors and forms the content of his work. Zola said that a work of art is a portion of nature seen through the temperament of the artist. But the work is accomplished by the employment of materials and media whose character also is exhibited in the total composition, in its style. And the portion of nature that is the subject matter of the work expressed in its content makes its own demands on the style. One can see, then, that style is a more comprehensive and subtle thing than form. One can isolate the form from the work of art and characterize it without quite saying all there is to be said about the style. So I suggest that style is a sort of higher-order timbre which stands to the whole composition as the (lower-order) timbre of the single note stands to the whole instrument it is played on. The style is thus an over-all form quality, and by it you identify the artist in the work and perhaps even the period, as you identify a person by the timbre of his voice. The form is a more restricted concept, as exemplified in Cézanne's "Boy in a Red Waistcoat" and "Mont Sainte-

Victoire"; these are different in form, but the style is unmistakably Cézanne's in both.

However, the concept of form in art is itself a subtle thing, and may be not unnaturally stretched to coincide with that of style, as when the artist is said to have found himself by changing from one style of composing to another. "Style" here could mean "form," if the form itself is ready-made and so may be experimented with. In this sense, we also speak of stylizing a performance or composition—making it conform to a recognized pattern. Meyer Schapiro has said some wise things about this in his essay on style.[14] A. C. Bradley has also said some wonderful things about form in relation to the medium and the content of a work of art, and about all these in relation to the subject matter outside.[15] So has Bosanquet,[16] but his insights are marred by a background commitment to a spiritualistic or idealistic theory of ultimate reality.

But for all that, the concept of fusion presents difficulties not resolved in the account above. These are spawned mostly by the ambiguities of the term. Just what fuses with what, and how, will become clearer as we proceed.

Expression and representation   About a page ago, I deliberately used the phrase ". . . subject matter of the work of art expressed in its content." If I had said ". . . represented by its content" instead, I would have been as well understood—or as much misunderstood. The reason for the option is that the term "represent," as far as it has any aesthetic relevance or use at all, is indeed hard to distinguish from "express." And the main reason for this is that representation in art cannot be mere representing (in duplicate, so to speak), or mirroring, or copying. It cannot be even imitating, unless you stretch the meaning of that term beyond recognition, as Aristotle tended to do, and as Eric Auerbach did.[17] Finally, the reason for this impossibility is that the artist has to have his say in his medium. The medium is his language, making its own demands.

A mirror is not a medium. When you see something in a good mirror, you are seeing *that thing* via the mirror. What is seen thus remains pure subject matter (except for certain reversals right to left,

---

[14] "Style," *A Modern Book of Esthetics*, ed. Melvin Rader (New York: Holt, Rinehart & Winston, Inc., 1960), pp. 336–48.

[15] "Poetry for Poetry's Sake," *Oxford Lectures on Poetry*, 2nd. ed. (London: Macmillan and Co., Ltd., 1920); selections in *A Modern Book of Esthetics*, pp. 309–23.

[16] "The Aesthetic Attitude in Its Embodiments," *Three Lectures on Aesthetics* (London: Macmillan and Co., Ltd., 1915); selection in *A Modern Book of Esthetics*, pp. 222–27.

[17] Eric Auerbach, *Mimesis* (Princeton: Princeton University Press, 1953).

which some artists exploit by holding their paintings up to a mirror to study the considerable difference in aesthetic values in the reversed image of the painting). There is no content in the mirror because there is no visible material and medium; thus there is no work of art, for nothing has been formulated in a medium as the content. Art is most certainly not a mirror held up to nature for the sake of the mirror-image. A mirror-image is not embodied in a medium that has certain opacities in its own right. One does not look into or through the medium of a work of art at the subject matter as one indeed does through or into a glass. In art, the subject matter undergoes some sort of trans-figuration when it is realized as the content in the medium. Even through colored glass, it is the subject matter that is seen as such, not as content. Thus the notion of transparency of the medium is misleading; vehicle of transfiguration is better.

Aesthetic representation has a history precisely because it is not a passive reflection of ready-made things as in a mirror. It is a constructive re-presentation, with the subject matter manifested as the content of the work of art. And how the artist does this depends partly on how he looks at things, which itself is a schematizing affair under categories that structure the field of experience this way or that. So we have the phenomenon of categorial aspection and the kind involving the lampshade or truncated pyramid.

All this makes the term "represents" in the art anything but equivalent to "corresponds to, by virtue of similarities." Its distinction from "expresses" thus becomes problematic. Yet, some works of art are undeniably representational, others are not. So some difference must be recognized and preserved between representational art and non-representational art, without loss of expressiveness in either case. Let us turn now to this delicate task of discrimination and characterization.

Some quick things might be said right away in the general terms we have introduced and examined above. For example, one could say that a work of art whose design requires that it be seen *as* something—this being the image content of the work—is in so far representational, whether the subject matter as such exists or not external to the work. And the composition is said to be nonrepresentational in so far as the content it features is without an explicit image. Both these sorts are expressive, however, as aesthetic objects. But there are some compositions whose content, if any, is so minimal—they have neither emotion nor image—that we say of them that they are purely formal, meaning that the expressive function is minimized. If such a work is a work of art, it satisfies certain formal requirements of the deployment of the elements of the medium. Since these elements, even linear ones, have their own aesthetic or timbre character, their proper formal arrangement may constitute an effective presentation and elucidation of the properties of aesthetic space without expressing anything. An expositor of Kandinsky once said rhetorically that some of his later compositions "express the essence of space." This will do if "express" is replaced by "present for prehensive perception," and "space" is qualified by "aesthetic." (There are spaces, and there are spaces.) Mondrian is another example. A fugue in music is a corresponding example; it presents for auditory prehension the architectonic of the aesthetic volume of the composition. There are space men among artists. They explore the properties of aesthetic space; they simply like to be in it.

Elucidating "representation" and "expression" this way makes representation and expression functional parts of the work itself. This is different from saying that the *artist* expresses himself or represents the subject matter—just *his* emotion, *his* image. The work of art itself is expressive or representational, independently of the artist's initial intention, though what he intended to do usually has some relation to the result. In the last chapter, we shall speak at greater length of the artist's intentions.

But it is also clear by now that restrictions must be put, by stipulation, on the use of "represent" and "express." One has to do this for precise aesthetic analysis. The terms are ambiguous, vague, and open-textured; [18] this is why they are so useful.

A step toward greater precision may be made by distinguishing between "descriptive portrayal" and "expressive portrayal," and then breaking the latter down into different kinds. By reference to the different kinds we can make the further distinctions necessary to philosophical aesthetics.

The first example of the difference between expressive and descriptive portrayal has no special relevance to the aesthetic case. Consider a good aerial photograph of a bit of terrain that is to be bombed. This certainly corresponds to something, and in that relationship, its whole value or meaning depends on the correspondence. Moreover, it is in effect a part of a set of instructions or directives as to what to do to the original; it is like an architect's blueprint that regulates the manipulation of building materials. Looked at this way, the photograph is a descriptive portrayal. It refers to something beyond it, where the description includes what is to be done about this referent. Of course, it could be severed from this use and be a descriptive portrayal still, as a direct report of the qualities of the referent itself, never minding what to do about it. But this is unusual.

After it is used, the photograph may be looked at reminiscently.

[18] Friedrich Waismann, "Verifiability," *Logic and Language*, 1st series, ed. Antony Flew (New York: Philosophical Library, 1951), pp. 117–44.

It then serves as a reminder of the experience or of that sort of situation, even for one who has not been through that particular experience, or who is reminded—or just minded—of similar situations that perhaps never existed. The picture then is the point of departure into fancy or reverie. A musical composition may also be this sort of occasion to get beyond the composition through what a composer has recently called autobiographical listening. Looking at a picture in this manner is still treating it as a "descriptive portrayal." We shall use the term that way. In this sense, a portrayal is descriptive when it is *attended by*—not expressive of—all sorts of images and feelings, without its being a work of art. But that is not the interesting point. The important point is that even a work of art, an excellent one, may function or serve as a descriptive portrayal, like the aerial photograph, for most people. But then we must find grounds for saying that these persons, in that rapport, mistake the work of art for something it is not. They fail to get its *own* sense. What I am saying is that taking something as a descriptive portrayal, even though it can be so used, is not a sufficient condition of its *being* a descriptive portrayal.

What, then, are the grounds for the contention that people who take a work of art for a descriptive portrayal are making a mistake? To answer this, we need the concept of expressive portrayal.

Let us get back to looking at the old, damp, granite wall that Leonardo da Vinci mentioned, with (let us say) its slate grays, gunmetal blues, and green-stained browns in what, for observation, is a random array of rough-edged patches, all in a flat plane except for slight unevennesses of the surface. But the wall is not simply, or in itself, a physical object. It is a material thing, a potential for realization either as an aesthetic or a physical object (categorial aspection). Its (basic) extension and other properties may readily be the occasion for seeing in it "divine landscapes, adorned with mountains, ruins, rocks, woods, great plains, hills, and valleys in great variety. . . ." [19] This is what it is if it becomes animated with aspects. To see it this way is to prehend it, whereupon the colored shapes become a medium the elements of which are distanced from one another by their intrinsic tone values *and* by what they are seen as; that is, the content—a landscape to Leonardo—thanks to the shapes.

Suppose, then, that this is the way you are looking at it, and that you wish to portray what we see. An ordinary photograph of the wall will not do, not even in color and in great detail. Such a descriptive portrayal would simply represent the wall. If someone is beside you, you might try a verbal portrayal of the mural landscape you prehend,

[19] Leonardo da Vinci, *Treatise on Painting* (London: George Bell & Sons, Ltd., 1877); quoted by Gombrich, *op. cit.*, p. 188.

pointing at the parts of the granite you are seeing as this or that and saying, "See the precipice here, and beneath it a dark lake in the shadow," outlining the figures with your finger as you speak. This line of talk might reveal to your companion what you see in the material confronting both of you, and yet it might not. Whether it did or not would be decided for you by his verbal response, in the form perhaps of a cry of recognition and his going on to point out other features of the landscape you had missed, all in the granite wall.

One thing seems clear about such a portrayal: it is not a description. You are not simply observing an object and reporting its qualities. But you are portraying something in a way that helps another to see what you see. You portray aspects that animate something, not qualities that qualify something. I say "see," not just "imagine." You are not imagining that portions of the stone are so-and-so. You *see* them *as* so-and-so. You could do the imagining with your eyes shut, but not the prehensive seeing. Nor does such seeing involve a projection of an image into the material; the material, as an aesthetic object featuring its medium, exhibits it for prehension. "But this isn't *seeing!*"—"But this *is* seeing!"—Wittgenstein said it must be possible to give both remarks a conceptual justification, and asked, "*In what sense* is it seeing?" [20]

Such is the sort of portrayal I am calling "expressive." Taking Leonardo's wall, you could more effectively portray what you prehend, you could express what you see, if, as an artist, you used the materials of your art in a composition that would present, more luminously than the original material thing and your talk about it, the figures obscurely discerned in it. The sketch or painting clearly embodies and portrays, without the help of talking, what may be just discernible in the original material. The better formulation of the content (aspect) in the medium of art is the job and the joy of the artist. So, as Leonardo went on to say, the artist likes to look at confused shapes in clouds or muddy water so that they will kindle him to make a creative composition in which they are realized. Or as Wittgenstein suggested, the artist produces something—the work of art—that is not to be vacillatingly seen as this or that, like the damp granite or the duck-rabbit figure, but to be regarded as something definite. The finished work of art is regarded as the subject matter expressively depicted in it.

The resulting work of art is an expressive portrayal, the logic of which is discussed in the last chapter. It might still be taken for a descriptive portrayal, as when it is looked at for what it reminds one of, but then it is being mistaken. The mistake breeds curious predica-

---

[20] Ludwig Wittgenstein, *Philosophical Investigations* (Oxford: Basil Blackwell, 1953), p. 203.

ments for any philosophy of art that works with an inadequate concept of portrayal of the expressive sort.

Of course, the nonplastic media of music and language may also be employed for purposes of expressive portrayal, or may be arranged to exhibit aspects that animate the medium instead of to describe qualities of the subject matter. This brings us into head-on collision with the question of representational and nonrepresentational works of art, a question that bears also on the plastic arts. After all, some works of art are "likenesses" in some sense of the term.

The details of this issue will be treated in the next chapter. At present let me put forth a schematic suggestion of what representation is in art.

In view of the fact that no work of art as an aesthetic object functions as a descriptive portrayal, such representation as it does achieve will be of a nondescriptive sort. It must be an expressive sort of representation. This chart indicates the right general distinctions:

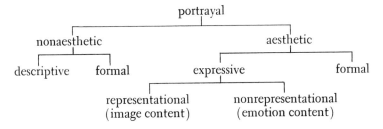

In its nonaesthetic modes, portrayal is descriptive and formal. Descriptive portrayal has subvarieties that we ought not to consider here at any length. The difference between descriptive and formal portrayal is the difference between the statements "cattle occasionally get hoof-and-mouth disease" (or a photograph used in such a description), and "the sum of the angles of a plane triangle equals two right angles" (or a triangular drawing used to illustrate this).

In its aesthetic modes, portrayal is expressive and formal. The expressive mode, in general, exhibits what the portrayal means in the medium of the expression; it breaks down into the representational and the nonrepresentational modes. Even representation here, notice, is a mode of expression. A work of art is representational when it exhibits an image content that expresses the subject matter, and there is a readily discernible likeness between properties of the materials arranged in its design and the properties of the subject matter as such. This likeness is the occasion for seeing the original (subject matter) depicted in the medium of the work as its content, although this resemblance itself is not seen or noticed in the aesthetic experience; it is not part of the object of prehension. On the other hand, a work of art is nonrepresentational when the image content—visual or auditory—expressing the subject matter in the medium does not depend so clearly on the sort of likeness mentioned above (titles help in such cases) and the image evinces emotion.

Examples of the difference between representational and nonrepresentational expression, both of which are expressive portrayals, can be arranged along a gamut between extremes, with intermediate examples that satisfy the conditions of both kinds of expression. Of the intermediate examples we would say that they are representational with respect to image content and nonrepresentational with respect to the emotion it evinces. Thus, in general, musical and verbal works of art are on the nonrepresentational side because properties of their materials are so unlike properties of the subject matter, except for occasional onomatopoeic likenesses. And, again in general, the plastic arts (excluding architecture) have a greater capacity for representation, for expressing the subject matter in the medium by virtue of image content, thanks to certain likenesses of materials and subject matter.

A work of art is formal in so far as it lacks a content of any sort; lacking this, it will also have no subject matter, since the content is the subject matter expressed in the medium of the work. But it will have a medium, formulated in an abstract way that makes the work's style of composition the main exhibit. This manner of composing, exhibited in formal works of art, takes the place of content. The elements of the medium, thus arrayed, determine and show the aesthetic space of the work, which is its whole point. This is a work of art in its simplest terms. "A picture in its simplest terms is something that fills a space," says Maurice Grosser [21]—aesthetic space, of course. The same may be said of any work of art in which the elements of form preempt the field of the composition. Such a work of art does not depend for its aesthetic merit on either representation or expression, even when it does happen to express or represent something. The content, if any, will be eclipsed by the form.

Speaking of form and expression in this general vein, and remembering what we said about style in connection with form on p. 46, we are prepared to extend the concept of expression into two other senses not yet recognized here but latent in much aesthetic talk. In order to do this effectively, let us first summarize and slightly amplify what has been said about the factors of a work of art: (1) the *materials* or instruments, primary and secondary (pigment and brush); (2) the *manner* of operating with these; (3) the *medium*, comprising the values or tonalities (timbres) of the primary instruments; (4) the *content*,

[21] Grosser, *op. cit.* (Mentor edition, 1956), p. 172.

which is the (5) *subject matter* expressively portrayed for prehension in the medium—what the painting is seen as; and (6) the *form*, which is (*a*) the array of the elements of the medium in aesthetic space, or (*b*) the pattern of the content or image realized in the formulated medium (for example, a frightened, crouching human being), and (*c*) the way in which the array of the elements of the medium and the pattern of the content cooperate to "form" the whole composition. Thus we speak of "first-order," "second-order," and "third-order" form. These distinctions will be clarified in applications made throughout the rest of the book.

This unity or third-order form, I suggested, has its own sort of timbre or tonality, and I identified this as the style of the work of art. It exhibits even the manner of composing and therefore the temperament of the artist, somewhat as the timbre of a note on a violin expresses the character of the whole instrument. This latter use of "express"—the character of the instrument "expressed" in the timbre— is not recognized in the treatment above. I shall here introduce it and speak of it as "first-order expression." Then "second-order expression" will be the sort already dealt with, more central to the work of art as an aesthetic object and pertaining to the transfiguration of subject matter into content of the work. Finally, there is the "third-order expression," which is the sense in which a style is expressive of so much. It is worth noticing the sort of correlation there is between this three-fold distinction and the similar one above of three orders of "form."

In this general account of expression and representation in art are echoes of such theories as Rudolf Arnheim [22] and Wittgenstein [23] have developed. Arnheim attacks subjectivism and associationism, favoring instead the notion that "the substance of the work of art [what we have called its expressive content] consists in what appears in the visible pattern itself. . . . The columns of a temple do not strive upward . . . because we put ourselves in their place, but because their location, proportion, and shape are carefully chosen in such a way that their image contains the desired expression." [24] He asserts that "expression is the primary content of vision" even in ordinary perceptual experience—the data are not bare lines and colors and sounds—and this feature is enhanced in "the way the artist looks at the world."

Arnheim's theory lacks the notion of "aspection," categorial and otherwise, a deficiency that Wittgenstein makes up for, but through subtle suggestion only. Developing such suggestions into the phe-

[22] *Art and Visual Perception* (Berkeley: University of California Press, 1957), Selection in *A Modern Book of Esthetics*, pp. 258–70.
[23] Ludwig Wittgenstein, *op. cit.*
[24] Arnheim, *loc. cit.*

nomenology of a material thing as a work of art, and of the mode of perception (prehension) relevant to its manifestation as an aesthetic object, has been the aim of the first and second chapters of this book.

The aim of the following two chapters is to detail and illustrate the general philosophical concepts. Moreover, the account above, as it stands, needs certain modifications. For example, the chart of expression and representation in art has the disadvantage of not allowing us to speak of a formal work of art as nonrepresentational, but the chart even as it stands suggests an answer to this. And there has been up till now an ominous by-passing of the art of letters, its materials (if any), and its medium. We shall try to work out such difficulties in what follows.

Finally, there is the hitherto untouched question of the definition of "work of art." I am saving that for the last chapter on art criticism. When an art critic gets to work assessing something, he wants to make sure it is a work of art. Then will be the time to wonder about the definition, which is after all a question for the logic of criticism.

THE ARTS

3

Architecture and sculpture   Schopenhauer, in *The World as Will and Idea,* constructed a magnificent philosophy of the arts which ordered them hierarchically. At rock bottom (literally!) is the art of architecture, which presents the forms of basic natural forces, the stresses and strains of matter in the field of space and gravitation. It harmonizes these best in the Classic style; Gothic architecture is confused. And so on up through sculpture, painting, poetry, and music, which more and more, in that order, express the human predicament in an ultimately irrational reality, from which art is an escape and a relief.

It is not the fashion any longer to do philosophy of art in that dramatic, metaphysical way, though vestiges of it are discernible in current theories. For example, what Kenneth Clark says about the almost cosmic significance of the human form in the nude at the peak of the hierarchy of forms [1] is rather like Schopenhauer's (and Hegel's) conception (see Clark's chapter, "The Naked and the Nude"). Still, we shall bow to the present fashion of requiring a less systematic treatment and, while borrowing something like the order in which the different arts are taken up in the old scheme, shall make some innovations even there. So we begin with architecture and sculpture. Such a beginning is still fairly popular among philosophical aestheticians. But we do this now without supposing that these arts are metaphysically basic.

In an important sense, buildings are not utilities like bridges,

[1] Kenneth Clark, *The Nude* (New York: Pantheon Books, Inc., 1956; also New York: Doubleday & Company, Inc., 1959, Anchor Book, A168).

56

cars, and pots and pans. We live and work *in* buildings. Where these are houses to live in, they provide place and local habitation for our persons, much as our bodies house our spirits. Notice how a sound body functions: it is a transparent means of access for environing nature and other people, while as a mask, it serves also to preempt an area of privacy for the animating mind. So for a house that is a home. It houses the whole person including his body and mind. It functions as a sort of acquired body. And if it is architecturally right, the domestic "inner" and the environing "outer" will be organically related while providing for the privacy of domestic life.[2]

The moral of all this is that a house that is a home is a place to live in, and is therefore a portion of *Lebensraum* (life-space). It is room for living. It is the "inner" of the housed person's consciousness. Such vital roominess is rhythmic and dynamic, an organic unity, unlike physical space. A good architect of a home will therefore compose a house that articulates these properties of *Lebensraum* instead of decomposing it by simply using walls to separate room from room or the whole house from the outside. Yet each wall will yield the right sort of privacy on both sides, a functional demarcation.

"Functional" architecture, so much spotlighted of late, is determined not only by function in the sense of "purpose," but even more by the materials of the building. The architect is an artist, and like any great artist, he loves his materials. He will therefore want these to show through in the finished "functional" work of art. In fact, the form he gives the building will be designed in large part to exhibit the character of the materials and what can be done with them in a composition that shows their nature in this sense of "function." This is a major reason why architectural forms have had a history. So now we have the skyscraper above and the groundling home below with its cantilevers affording sheltered spaces without walls or supporting pillars.

Architecture is a formal art, and in this there is a temptation for the great architect as artist. Of course, he is also necessarily an engineer and a human being, but as an artist he is tempted to use his technical understanding of material stresses and strains primarily to produce a composition that does more justice to the organic unity of room with room and of the whole building with its site, than to the "function" of the building as a home, a place to live in. This imbalance has recently made many a *house* more at home on its site than it has the *occupant* at home in the house, unless the occupant is himself more a formal artist than one who must live and work at something else. Some of Frank Lloyd Wright's houses exemplify this, though it was Wright himself who said that the nature of the

[2] Frank Lloyd Wright, *The Natural House* (New York: Horizon Press, 1954).

"entire performance" should be determined with a view to both "the nature of the materials and the nature of the purpose".[3] In other words, this functionalism tends to result in a formal work of fine art in aesthetic space, to be appreciated more by the purely aesthetic sense— as an abstract statue or picture—than by the domestic sense for the properties of *Lebensraum*. The truly great architect will know how to satisfy the demands of both the aesthetic sense and the sense of a good place to live or work in. In short, he will remember that an architect is not just an artist. As an architect he is also an artisan whose finished work is to be an abode of the human spirit, or of the divine spirit if it is a church. The work will therefore realize the nature of the spirit along with the nature of the materials and the aesthetics of their formal organization.

Le Corbusier is an example of a good architect who, on occasion, remembers the "function" of architecture in both these senses—and who also forgets. The house he built for Hélène De Mandrot at Le Pradet in France was a simple rectangular thing built partly of local rubble and by local village craftsmen, not on the supporting pillars for which he had become famous. Thus there was an intimate tie-in with the natural and social environment.[4] Perhaps he conceded too much to common humanity with this house, reacting against the principle of dehumanization in pure art. But in another famous instance Le Corbusier leaned too far the other way, toward sculptural effect. This is his Notre-Dame-du-Haut (Ronchamp, France, 1950–1954), which invites judgment as statuary rather than as architecture.[5] Unfortunately it suggests a Dutch head with a hat; it even has eyes and mouth. This is not the way for a church to provide place and local habitation for the divine spirit and the congregation of worshipping spirits; it tempts one to look at it, rather, as a mammoth statue.

This borderline case is the bridge on which we pass over into a brief consideration of sculpture. We have noticed about architecture that, in so far as it is an art at all, it is primarily formal. Strictly speaking, it has neither content nor subject matter as an art. And it is an "impure" art, not in the sense of combining several arts (as does opera, for example) but in the more radical sense of having a leg outside the whole field of art proper. Architecture has artisanship built into it. What distinguishes architecture from sculpture is the fact that the latter has, in addition, both subject matter and content. The art of sculpture is allied with architecture by virtue of the ma-

[3] Frank Lloyd Wright, *The Future of Architecture* (New York: Horizon Press, 1953), p. 13.

[4] Henry Russell Hitchcock, *Architecture: Nineteenth and Twentieth Centuries* (Baltimore: Penguin Books, Inc., 1958).

[5] *Ibid.*, p. 387 and Plate 167.

terials. These are pretty much the same for both arts—wood, stone, metal, and clay—and this constitutes a close alliance, with the temptations naturally attending such affinities. In view of this, one understands the trespassing and the resulting borderline cases.

Because of this affinity of materials, buildings naturally have much sculpturing—friezes, relief, and full statues emerging out of the walls or columns or even serving as pillars. But statuary is nothing if not more picturesque than architecture. It is more representational, and therefore with a greater capacity for expression, in the restricted sense specified before. A statue is to be seen and felt as something, unlike a building howsoever artistically composed.

So sculpture has emerged as a separate art and a *fine* art. A "fine" art is concerned primarily with the manipulation of plastic materials for the sake of the animation of the medium by a content. (Material, medium, content; remember that these are separate concepts.)

Though the tints and the textures of the materials employed by the sculptor are of considerable importance, they are secondary to the form of the finished work, "form" here having much to do with shape given the sculptured material. The sculptor will select textures **and** tints not for their own sakes, but with a view to the way they are related to the illumination of the figure. The way the figure receives and gives back light is important for the form it is to have in aesthetic space, when prehended as something. When this happens, it is primarily the shape of the figure that is transfigured into the medium of the work of art, animated by the content. (The form is the chief carrier of content in sculpture.) Then it is the form of what the statue is prehended as, the form, in aesthetic space, of the content— a man erect, a reclining panther. The statue is then no longer a piece of stone or bronze or wood simply with the shape of a man or a panther; it is a panther or a man "in" stone, wood, or bronze, the content animating it into an aesthetic object. The point of statuary, in general, is that one may do one's imagining or have his images, not just in his mind, but out there in the artistic configurations of materials that are made to accommodate them.

Sculpture honors its materials in two ways: by presenting clear likenesses half buried in the material (Rodin's "La Pensée," less well known than "Le Penseur"), or by massive suggestion of a figure that leaves the material as palpable as the form itself (Ahron Ben-Shmuel's "Seated Woman"). The statues of Henry Moore, especially his more recent ones, achieve a similar effect by abstraction and unlikeness. The surface textures are left rough. But when an artist makes abstractions, he is usually featuring form above material. An abstract composition is more for the sake of the form than for the sake of either the material or of expressiveness. However, some expressiveness is retained by a title for the work—"Reclining Figure," for example— suggesting the subject matter that it may be prehended as. The featuring of form, almost to the point of liberating it from the material, is exemplified in Brancusi's well-known "Bird in Space." (The title saves this from being a purely formal composition; curiously, *with* this title, the figure comes to life as a bird, and a bird only; options to seeing it as anything else seem eliminated.)

Therefore, the sculptor's love of his materials must not be exaggerated. As an artist, he is a composer in aesthetic space, where it is primarily the formulated medium and the expression that count. Most statues obviously exhibit this complex concern as the primary one.

Painting and photography   A man depicted in stone is significantly different from a man depicted in a picture. The man in stone seems less problematic because the stone, even as just material, has a bulk by virtue of which it can accommodate (embody) the image, providing for an easier coincidence of the shape of such material with the form of the petrified image. (Yet even here a difference remains: the second-order form of what the statue is seen as—the image content—is never identical with the shape of the material.) But a picture, as pigment on canvas or photographic print, seems to be curiously stretched and inflated by the content or image, at least to some epistemologists of art. So the misleading analogy with looking through a window pane at something or seeing it in a mirror is suggested as an alleged solution to the problem, the suggestion being that we are not really looking at the picture when we prehend the voluminous image; we are conscious of something *through* it instead of *in* it. Yet, notice that when the imagination stretches the material (strictly, the medium) of the picture looked at in the usual way, this stretching is quite different from the sort of extension the picture gets when it is viewed through a stereoscope. We properly speak of the illusion of depth and solidity in a stereoscope because the picture thus blown up looks more like a statue or the real thing, and this is certainly a mere appearance. Such solidity is quite different from that of, say, the apples in a still life by Cézanne, who was not aiming at illusory stereoscopic effects.

From the web of intriguing considerations that can be teased out of such phenomena I shall feature only one, to show the sense in which pictures, though static like statues, are closer to music and poetry than statues are. It concerns the way in which the aesthetic space of the composition is determined and the form of the image content. In a statue, the shape of the material counts for more. In a picture, the shape of the material still counts—the shape of the sketched or pigmented patches—but only as contour. Thus the voluminousness or solidity (form) of the image content of the pictorial work of art is freer, less determined by the shape of the material. This puts more of a premium on color and light and shade which now, in the absence of a solid material, collaborate with contours to determine the form of the content in the aesthetic space of the picture. Much modern painting is done primarily to exhibit the power of colors to determine aesthetic first-order form, without much reliance even on contour.

So, since form is thus molded also by colors in a picture, the space of a picture as aesthetic object is freer than a statue's and is thus a more appropriate milieu for detailing the content or giving it nuances of the sort that would spoil a statue. In this sense, a picture may be more expressive of its subject matter than a statue may be. With this freer aesthetic space of the picture goes a liability. It tempts the aesthetically uneducated imagination to read into the picture space what is not really there. Statue space is not so tempting in this respect, especially if the statue is a good one. A picture can be a good one and still incite the wrong response, because of the nature of picture space. Modern and recent painters have taken to painting in a way that reduces this liability.

We shall see that it is this space feature that makes a picture more like poetry and music than a sculptural work of art is.

There is a sense in which the artist experiences things with the instruments (materials, primary and secondary) of his art. Thus the educated eye of a painter does not see things quite the way in which the educated eye of the photographer does. The photographer sees with camera and film; the painter with brush and pigment. This means that each tends, when he has mastered the instruments, to see even the original thing as it will look in the medium of the finished work of art. And how it will look there depends on the tonalities of the instruments and on how he manipuates them.

One may say that the camera and the processing of the film stand to the developed film as the brush and brushing stand to the deployed pigment on canvas. There is such a thing as using a camera relative to the film as one uses a brush relative to the pigment, and of getting the feel of one as of the other. Great photographers have avowed this in books and magazines on the art of photography. And the artist who has engaged in both arts has sensed how his accomplishment in one tends to detract from his capacity in the other. This is because he learns to see things with the materials of the art, and these are different in the two cases. (Similarly, proficiency in badminton will spoil your tennis, because greater wrist action is required by the lighter and more aerial instruments.)

Composing with a camera, if it is not in a studio, is an affair of waiting upon or for the right dispositions of things and their illuminations. (See some desert shots with a low sun for shadows, by E. Weston.) Such waiting may involve moving the camera into the right position, for the right pattern of bright and dark areas from that point of view. Then the processing may be used to enhance or subdue the brights and darks. The resulting composition may, under such controls, be an abstraction, in the sense of featuring forms or masses beyond what is found in the state of nature; and any artist working with any material must abstract in some way and to some degree. Since the camera does not give him control over color sufficient for free sculpting with it—molding form thereby—he can better achieve his abstraction or formulation by black-and-white photography. The greatest triumphs of the photographic art are therefore black-and-white photographs, and the great photographer prefers these. The absence of color here helps, as in sculpture. The main point in all this is that the camera can be used as an instrument of pictorial expression, with more than just stark image content factually recording the subject matter. Alfred Stieglitz was the first great photographer to announce and defend this thesis, devoting his magazine *Camera Notes* to this end. However, Stieglitz was as much concerned to say that photography, because of its distinctive instruments, is a separate art, not to be judged by the standards of either drawing or painting.[6]

The great life shots must not be overlooked. The excellence of these is judged by still another standard, that of story telling and detailed representation, where, of course, this is still expressive portrayal in so far as it has any aesthetic merit and not just descriptive merit. A good life shot is to be regarded as something, in a prehension of the content and form of the photograph as an aesthetic object.

Yet, photography remains a minor art because of the limitation of the instrument—the insufficiently constructive control it gives the artist over details of color and form. So we do not frame a photograph, however great in its own way, and price it at half a million dollars, as we do a painting. Photography is less creative, less constructive, and therefore less "expressive" for what that means in art. This is because it puts a machine between the artist and his finished work, one that tends to do too much of the picturing on its own. *It* takes the picture in a way that a brush and pigments by themselves do not. These do not comprise a machine to be operated. So

[6] Beaumont Newhall, *Photography*, rev. ed. (New York: Museum of Modern Art, 1938), pp. 63ff.

we speak of the camera eye, more often than of the photographer's eye. (Nor is a piano or a violin a machine in the sense in which a camera is; they are to be handled more as a brush than a camera.) There is a moral in this for the present-day painter. Let him beware of taking to his art with mechanical tools such as pressure-brushes that spray on the paint. One must feel more intimately the hand of the painter in the painting, among the other things prehended in it. Thus does the painting get its style, which involves among other things the temperament of the artist, and this is concentrated in the brush-in-hand as he paints. The brush stroking is a kind of manual dance which impresses the composition with the form and content of the artist's prehension. For example, Matisse's brush-in-hand dances in aerial brush strokes in front of the canvas before the brush touches it for the animating application of the pigment.

Some paintings emphasize only one or a few of the five or six features that constitute the nature of a work of art—materials, medium, form, and the others. Let us see how this works out, remembering that a painting is basically a material thing that one may love, not simply a physical object, which is precisely how the material thing appears when an affectionate rapport with it is excluded on principle. (Of course, neither is it simply an aesthetic object, as we have noticed; in fact, prehending it that way also excludes loving it, a point I shall return to later on.)

What the painter loves he tends to celebrate in one way or another in his work of art. It must in some way or other show through in the composition. Suppose he loves his materials—brush, canvas, and paints. Then the brushing will show through in brush strokes, the rhythm and direction of which are left visible in the finished work. This will also draw attention to the paint as applied *pigment*, not color. And the texture of the canvas will remain on exhibit in thin applications, with even its original white showing through here and there in a sprinkle of untinctured dots. Cézanne painted a self-portrait this way, in a mood of loving his instruments more than himself. Of course, more than just the instruments and their use is exhibited in the painting, or else it would not count as a work of art. But let us say that in such cases —clearer-cut ones may be found—the materials of the art are featured. And this can be done effectively by a master.

Where this happens, a restriction must be made: we must deny that the materials thus exhibited are proper parts of the painting as an aesthetic object. They function rather to preserve the sense of its ground in the instruments, or of its reality as a beloved material thing. Modern and recent painters have wanted to remind themselves and the world that, basically, they paint canvasses, not landscapes and people. Yet not quite as house painters paint houses.

To feature the medium of a painting is to concentrate on the timbres of the tones produced by the instruments. These are, we remember, a first-order expression of the character of the instruments or materials, the color timbre of pigments singly and in combination. These may be emphasized in a composition that draws attention away from the basic material to the medium as color textures. Subtle juxtapositions, and glazing and scumbling, of pigments will enhance these pure color effects, making this medium seem to veil the material in favor of itself as color texture-and-expanse. There is a strong trend towards this emphasis in mid-century painting.

Form is also given the spotlight in much modern painting. Of course, texture involves fine-grained patterns, but it is not until an over-all architectonic of the elements of the medium is realized in the aesthetic space of the picture that first-order form is being featured. Special recognition of form is achieved better by toning down the elements (color tonalities) of the medium in favor of their structural organization. Braque and Picasso in their cubistic periods provide good examples. Also, the content must be kept inconspicuous. In a Mondrian checkerboard type of painting, content is completely excluded. Trying to see it as something is a mistake. An example of a wonderful blend of form *and* medium, minimizing all else without obliterating it, is Delaunay's "Simultaneous Windows" a color-plate of which is in the third of the Skira volumes.

Content is featured when a composition transmutes the medium's tonalities and the first-order forms into characteristics of what the painting is seen as, or what is depicted in it. Thus the medium *per se* and first-order form *per se* become invisible in favor of the content with its second-order form—say, the smiling face of a middle-aged woman. Color here is "of the cheeks," and the form "of the face." In Rembrandt's "Portrait of Baartjen Martens" the content is featured thus, masterfully. In paintings that emphasize medium and form, the color tonality was the animation of the materials, the first-order form an expression of aesthetic space. But in Rembrandt's picture, tonality and second-order form combine to become the animation of a smiling face that, as the content of the picture, expressively portrays the external subject matter.

Subject matter, which is not as such a proper part of the work of art, is nakedly represented in paintings that tend not to be works of fine art. This is the other end of the spectrum from materials, which we have seen are also outside the work proper as an aesthetic object. A magazine cover girl is an example. Of course, even a good painting that celebrates content is indirectly emphasizing subject matter—the sitter for Rembrandt's portrait.

It is possible to paint a picture in which all these factors are featured separately and all at once: material, medium, form, content, and subject mater via content. For example, look at the plate of André Derain's "Still Life with a Jug," used as a frontispiece for this book. It plainly shows and celebrates the oil paints (materials), especially in the parallel brush strokes in the Cézanne manner at the lower left, and in the skillful overlaying of pigment on pigment. In the medium this shows up as sculptural or solid volumes defined and animated by muted color expanses—solid, yes, but shot through and softened with luminous color nuances, despite the suggestion of cubism. In this first-order form of the medium, the light-brown triangular area left of the dark turquoise of the jug protrudes toward the plane of the picture. But now see the medium thus structured as a still life with a jug. This tends to recess that color element into becoming a part of the table, back of the jug. Similar dynamic tensions are realized throughout the picture, especially in the area of the table cloth and what is next to it. Thus is the content realized with its second-order form; but in an expressive unity with the first-order form of the elements of the medium. These two factors make demands on one another that they mutually satisfy. The resulting composition expressively portrays not only the subject matter indicated by the title, but presents a space which also harbors an elemental affection for the staples of human life, as a part of the content. This fuses with the rest, in the over-all unity of third-order form which is the style of the painting, or of the painter at that period. Dérain's "Still Life with a Jug" is my favorite painting, and my inclination is to favor paintings done this way. This is to do everything that can be done in the art of painting, with an even emphasis on the various possibilities. Other types of paintings may be excellent, but by a selective featuring of only some of the five factors that are available to the art. The result of such extraction for favorable notice is abstraction. Even an over-realistic painting is "abstract" in this use of the term, since it underemphasizes medium and first-order form. There are no rules against this. Nevertheless, something is against it with a perennial, mute, and gentle force: the combined possibilities of the art. It is these together that make the abstractive omissions faddist or fashionable with periodic appeal only. But such exclusiveness serves a purpose, as we shall see in the next chapter.

Dancing, acting, and pantomime   A good dancer is a mobilized statue. It is not difficult to imagine a statue coming to life in a dance because so many statues already express a complete action, without the mobility of an actual dance. Bernini's "David" might well be imagined as coming out of that belligerent position into a sling dance, expressively

portraying David's fight with Goliath. Some statues have dance posi-
tions or tableaux explicitly built into them, as in Georg Kolbe's "Heine
Denkmal." [7] Thus dancing is fluid sculpture.

But the "coming to life" in a good dance will be under controls.
Too much personal expression in detailed facial contours—the appearance of talking or screaming—will spoil a statue even as a statue.
(See Pollaiuolo's "Hercules and Antaeus." [8]) A good dancer retains some
of the facial and other formal impassivities of a good statue. (It is
worth noticing, in passing, that even the best paintings of human
beings, portraits or not, also avoid representing the subject as talking
or screaming.)

The main point of the comparison is that the material of the
art of dancing is the body-in-action of the dancer, and that he will
formulate something with it in a pattern of actions that expressively
portrays something, as does a statue with its form alone or primarily.
But because of the mobility, the eventual form of the whole dance
will involve temporal and rhythmic elements that elaborate the
medium, giving it a spread in which almost any subject matter (theme)
can be expressed as the content of the enactment. But, even so, the
over-all third-order form of the completed dance retains something of
the statuesque, despite its extension or dynamic progression in time and
its freer aesthetic space. It remains a plastic art, to say the least.

Dancing is now usually a "performing art." That is, there is
the dance choreographically "written out" on the one hand and there
are its performances on the other. This means that the dancer is
generally not the composer of the dance he performs. Yet he composes, in a sense. There is more room for this in interpretive dancing
featuring a single dancer than in, say, ballet. In interpretive dance, the
dancer realizes the dance in an interpretive articulation, as the pianist
the musical composition, or the actor the play. In this connection, however, another point emerges for notice. One may say that, strictly,
the dancer's body is the material for the work of the composer, who,
as the creative artist, need not be the dancer. So he mobilizes human
bodies into formal patterns, male or female, somewhat as the sculptor
works on bronze. The dancer in the dance is the finished bronze
statue—the composer's work of art, not the dancer's. This is true
unless the dancer is the composer, composing as he dances, or himself
formulating it choreographically beforehand.

Dancing is usually done to music, and is then an impure art,
a mixture of two arts. Perhaps dancing is a minor art, as a hybrid
between sculpture and music. If you watch with a sculptor's eye

[7] T. M. Greene, *The Arts and the Art of Criticism*, p. 567 (plate).
[8] *Ibid.*, p. 573 (plate).

for plasticity, the pattern of forms presented by the action of the dance freezes into something statuesque, addressing itself to visual intelligence. If you listen with a musician's ear, the medium that carries the content of the dance is more for audition than vision; the visible forms are absorbed into the musical rhythms. Thus, candidates even for a dance are said to be given "an audition." Curiously, we do not speak of giving "a vision" in that way.

If the sculptural emphasis is made, the medium of the art of dancing becomes thin and elusive, hard to distinguish from the dynamically patterned material, as in the case of sculpture. The color tints of the body, or of its costume, still count for something, but this not as essential as the form, which is here more a function of the shapes of the deployed material than of the relationships of the color tones. But the sonorities of the elements of the music enrich the medium of the dance, thickening it so that it can carry a content of image and emotion in a way that sculpture cannot. Thus a dance can tell a story; it has a literary or programmatic content amplified by the pattern of the action of the dance if this is mimetic (imitative) and is not looked at with the sculptor's eye of a formalist. This is another impurity in the art of dancing. So one may see, listen to, and, let us say, "read" a dance, all three. Such impurities need not prevent the dance from being a great work of art. As long as it is composed and performed in a manner that does not distract attention from the content to the subject matter outside the dance, the artistry is unimpaired. The greatest dancers will not mind telling a story, provided it is exhibited as image and emotion content in the form—the sculptural and musical pattern of the dance—as in any great formal work of art. With this requirement in view, the good dancer will realize that it is not his job to express his own feelings in the dance. At a psychic distance from his own inner life, he molds the movements of his body into the significant forms that exhibit the content of the composition, never minding how *he* feels during the dance. This content may include an emotion or a mood, but the person of the dancer must be kept out of sight in the presentation of the content; his person must not be allowed to intrude into the picture in the formulated medium of the dance.

The dance at its best does not forget its primary affiliation with plastic art; it tends to minimize, or discard altogether, narrative content in favor of the fusion of sculptured movement and music. Anyone who sees the second acts of *Swan Lake* and *Giselle*, or Balanchine's *Agon*, or Martha Graham's *Celebration*, will realize this. The primary aim of the dance is not to portray what is personal about persons, not even what is personal about the persons expressively portrayed in the dance, if any.

Acting is a different affair. There the personal factor becomes supremely relevant. But again, never the actor's person or personality, except as the material of the performance, and this is outside what the dramatic work of art formally presents. The actor's personality, in addition to his body, is included in the material to be controlled, for the sake of what the actor in the play's action is to be seen as, the content of the play. In short, he is impersonating some other person, and that is how the personal counts in acting as a proper part of the drama. There are characters in the play, and it is their persons which are to be expressed or realized in the histrionic action on the stage of the theater. The fact that an actor must be carefully selected for a part with a view to his personality does not mean that the personality is going to be put on exhibit in the play. It means rather that since the material of the art of acting includes personal traits of the actor, care must be taken to choose such as can most aptly be molded in a good impersonation of the part or character to be played, as marble with the right tints will be selected by the sculptor. Of course, a great actor will know how to control his own person during the performance, getting a fine characterization of the part without much reliance on personal traits of any special sort, as the great sculptor will give you a fine figure out of almost any solid material that can be given a shape. But it helps to have the right material, too, as we saw earlier.

Speaking and gesture are of the essence in acting. This differentiates it from dancing and sculpture. Facial expression would also be important if it were visible by the spectator; the good actor, realizing that most of the spectators in the theater cannot see his grimaces or smiles, will make his speech and gestures do the smiling or grimacing as need be. Language may be used that way. So he will save his energies for that, instead of expending them on facial exercise. The reason that speaking is essential to the histrionic art is that the point of the art is primarily to present the character as concentrated in the manner and content of his talking. The primary action on the stage is therefore linguistic action in its root form, which includes gesture and posture. A painting, a statue, will show that the man or woman you see it as is thinking (Rodin's "Le Penseur"), or how the subject of the composition feels. It will not show you *what* he is thinking about, as the occasion for his action and passion. So there was need for an aesthetic medium which, when properly composed, reveals and specifies the inner life of the part played, in full-bodied action. And the most full-bodied action for a human being is linguistic action in its original setting, namely, speaking with all the gestures that are so integral to the primary use of language. (Remember what goes on in situations where the native tongue is being learned: the child is in the presence of people actively using the language.)

It is this that puts the histrionic art perhaps a little closer to the art of dancing than to literature. The body of the actor counts for so much, as the material. His personality also counts as material, as we have seen, but it is material for the full-bodied action concentrated in speech, which he engages in with his whole body-in-action.

The medium of the art is the sonorities of the language caught in the rhythmic pattern of the whole action. (This remark will have to be improved and sharpened in the discussion of the art of literature.) The playwright composes with this in view, and the actor cooperates with the composer in the performance of the play. The content of the dramatic action is the character which the actor is seen as, the person that the action expressively portrays, who is certainly different from the person of the actor.

The art of the mime is significantly different from the full-bodied art of dramatic acting. The mime cuts out the audible speaking. Acting without speaking is a truncated human action, so the mimetic art is a minor art. If a person is being impersonated in the imitative action, the point of the latter is to see how much of the character's speech can be suggested while the mime says nothing. Like Frans Reynders (of the Dutch school of mimes) in "A Man at a Table," he goes through the motions of talking only, and the spectators guess what is said. In such cases, there is such a thing as "getting the illusion of," and no great art is concerned with that. But where what is being presented in the mimetic action is not a human character, as in Reynder's "The Marionette" and "The Bird," the dumb show is just right, weaving a pattern that may be seen as a bird or a marionette, in a complete, genuine expressive portrayal of the subject matter. In fact, the mime has this single advantage over the full-fledged actor: he may properly act nonhuman parts, since speaking is ruled out. The limitation of pantomime is that it is most truly art only when the parts played are nonhuman.

But even the mime is not simply pretending to be something or to be doing something he is not. A *fortiori*, Laurence Olivier never pretends to be Hamlet. Acting is not pretending, and the great actors are not the great pretenders. The difference between the concept of pretending and the concept of acting is well worth study. A whole, adequate philosophy of art is suggested by the correct analysis of this. Of course, we do sometimes tell people to stop acting, meaning to tell them to stop pretending. "Acting" does also have that use. In this sense,

De Quincey spoke of actions "tainted with a false histrionic feeling." People acting that way are pretending with the intention of deceiving. They want you to think that they are something they are not. An actor aims at making you see him *as* a character which everybody knows he is not. There is no deception or illusion during the performance or afterwards. This is a vast difference, worth prolonged study. The country yokel, accustomed to holophrastic perception, overlooks the difference in the theater when he rushes towards the stage to prevent Othello from suffocating Desdemona.

These considerations of dancing, acting, and pantomime are incomplete without a closer consideration of the literature and the music that implement them, and that stand out each in its own right as a separate art.

Music   This treatment of the art of music is going to be a brief examination of a moot concept, that of the "form of a feeling." A decision concerning this will clarify the sense in which music may be representational or have a content somehow expressive of a subject matter.

Suzanne Langer has argued that the form of a work of art expresses a feeling or emotion, and that this form is the form of the feeling.[9] The artist, especially the musical artist, knows in a nonlogical way the nature of emotions, which is to have an intuitive grasp of their forms. It is these that he exhibits with the presentational immediacy of the art symbol, essentially the expressive form of the composition. Of course, Mrs. Langer distinguishes this sense of "form" from the several other senses of the term. So, to say the least, she does not mean the shape of a feeling by its "form." To articulate a feeling in a composition is to objectify it, and thus to convert it into the expressive form of the work for aesthetic prehension. This distinguishes such expression from nonaesthetic expression in the mere venting of feeling, in, say, an irate letter to someone, or in exclamations, ejaculations, or grunts—all cases of self-expression. Thus the artist need not express the feelings that he simply has as he composes, or had before, or will have. He is cognizant, rather, of the forms of feelings and puts the feelings on exhibit by virtue of their forms, in his compositions.

This statement suffers not so much from being simply wrong as from a failure to make a sufficient number of distinctions, thus leaving unanswered several pertinent questions. A similar judgment applies to Rudolph Arnheim's general theory of expression and expressive forms. Arnheim claims that there are emotionally expressive forms in

[9] Suzanne Langer, *Problems of Art* (New York: Charles Scribner's Sons, Inc., 1957); also a selection in *A Modern Book of Esthetics*, pp. 248–58.

nature even beyond the human; for example, that of a weeping willow which certainly cuts a drooping figure. There is an intrinsic sadness in such a form. The feeling is not there simply by association with human posture. It is a datum of prehensive perception, of the visual sort in this example.

Now let me move on from these thoughts in the direction of something they suggest. An aesthetically good musical expression of sadness will expressively portray the feeling without too close an imitation of a special case of a sad thing. That is, a musical composition that specifically portrays, say, a lamenting woman would have to resort to slavish, onomatopoeic configurations of sounds. As Langer says, it is the form of the feeling that counts, in music especially, more than the depiction of the particular thing that has or exhibits the feeling. This gets me to a heresy. I suggest that the dynamic form of the *auditory* image content of music may be identical with the form prehended in aesthetic *vision*. The sadness expressively portrayed in, say, the *adagio* movement of Bach's *E Major Concerto for Violin*, with its drooping figures, especially of the base in its counterpoint, is as much that of a weeping willow as of a human being, and one does not generally listen to a willow tree. So it is a mistake to suppose that music has its own variety of audible forms. The same form of the feeling may be prehended both in the auditory and the visual work of art. For example, to get the form of the feeling in a Käthe Kollwitz female figure is to prehend what is formulated in the sad drooping figures of a musical composition.

In view of this, I press in favor of the heresy that the content of a musical work is as visual as it is auditory—or strictly neither of these exclusively—and that it is an innocent and natural thing to do for the listener to supply some visual imagery which specifies the form of the feeling; though the specific image (a lamenting woman) will, of course, not be a proper part of the work. But its simply being visual will not count against the quality of the audition, since the form in question does not have a closer relation to being heard than to being seen, where both these are prehensive. Moreover, a corollary of this is also subversive of another adage in philosophy of art, to the effect that all art aspires to the condition of music. One might as well say that music aspires to the condition of all art. The truth about all art is that if it aims at expression at all—if it is not purely formal art—its aim is to realize in the medium a content that expressively portrays the subject matter, with the help of a formulation that does not address itself exclusively either to eye or ear. This is true even of impressionist painting, which is famous for its visual sensitivity. I believe it was Cézanne who said of Monet: "*Il n'est qu'un oeil, mais quel oeil!"* But no artist who captures expressive content in his work, with its second-order form, is *just* an eye, or just an ear, or just a heart, despite the difference in materials and media.

The nail of this idea, heretical to the purists [10] with their "pure listening" maxim, is driven in further with the hammer blow of another consideration concerning titles. This point is that a musical composition may be excellent on the formal count, and can therefore reward "pure listening," while nevertheless accommodating fairly specific imagery both auditory and visual, when bearing a title. This happens quite legitimately when the schematic second-order form of the content, realized with the help of the title, is in fact the form of whatever the composition is heard or seen as. (The drooping figure fits different sad particulars.) A good example of this is one of Johann Kuhnau's biblical sonatas for harpsichord, *Il Combattimento tra David e Goliath*. The style is baroque but not too much at the expense of form. One passage is such that, with the help of the title, it can be seen and heard as David's slingshot attack on Goliath, with dramatic detail. Even Beethoven wondered in his latter years if he should not have appended "poetical titles" to some of his pieces. (J. W. N. Sullivan,[11] in writing of Beethoven, argues against purely formal music which he calls "isolated," and against the opposite extreme of straight program music, while favoring the intermediate sort called "spiritual.")

Of course, the purist's complaint against impure listening, and the program music that induces it, is directed mainly at what one musician has called "autobiographical" listening (Paul Schwartz) which imports into the audition items from the listener's personal experience, images which are psychologically associated with the composition for the listener but not expressed by it or realized in its content for prehension by any perceptive listener. Such listening may have value as a pleasant pastime; it is more to be enjoyed as a reminder than as an expressive portrayal.

In this connection, music with verbal and histrionic accompaniments must not be overlooked. *Lieder* and operas, though impure in the sense of employing materials and media of various arts, may nevertheless thereby aesthetically incorporate more elaborate content in the composition. That is, a "pure listening" directed on these, selectively attending to formal features, would miss much of the content which is really there in the aesthetic spaces articulated by the performances. Getting the whole "story," which need not involve autobiographical

[10] E. Hanslick, *The Beautiful in Music* (New York: The Liberal Arts Press, Inc., 1957) selection in Weitz, *Problems in Aesthetics* (New York: The Macmillan Company, 1959), pp. 381–410.

[11] J. W. N. Sullivan, *Beethoven: His Spiritual Development* (New York: Alfred A. Knopf, Inc., 1927); also in *A Modern Book of Esthetics*, pp. 286–300.

listening, is even required by such impure art forms. So we read the libretto, preferably in advance of the performance.

There is another factor of form that has been understressed so far in this account. This is form as rhythm, a feature to be distinguished, not separated, from the form of images. Rhythm may be thought of as the form of movement or action, and much of the dynamism of a composition is attributable to its form in this sense. It is this that makes the content expressive of what is beyond both visual and auditory data as "fixed" images. To speak of "dynamic" images is implicitly to recognize the factor of rhythm. And it is this that links music with the other arts, more conspicuously the dance. If you feel or get the rhythm of a composition, howsoever formal, you will have the impulse to dance to it. Of course, if it is chamber music, the dancing will be sublimated into, say, slight head movements. I once sat behind an excellent composer of quite formal—sometimes atonal—pieces for string quartets. It was at the first performance of one of his compositions. I saw him dancing with his head and hands to the piece, though the listening was pure enough to keep the movements down to a minimum of visibility. I just barely detected them. The purists who smile at such a response as appropriate only for country yokels are taking on airs under the influence of a wrong principle, though there certainly is a difference on principle between music for dance and music for audition alone.

Having just mentioned verbal and rhythmic features, we are ready to turn inquiringly to the art of letters.

Literature   What are the materials and the medium? This question is most perplexing when directed at the literary art. And without an adequate conception of materials and medium in literature, the notions of its content and form are also too indefinite to be of much use. So our main effort now must be to sharpen up these concepts in connection with the art of letters. Some distinctions not commonly made must now be considered.

Let me begin *in medias res*, and let this bit of Latin mean "among the material things" related to the art of literature. Of course, material things may be relevant in two quite different ways: as subject matter (London, for example, in Blake's poem) and as materials. My chief concern is with the latter. What are the materials of the art?

This question is often not distinguished from the question about the *medium*, so a single, blanket answer is given to both: language. This lack of discrimination leaves other key concepts of the aesthetics of literature also in a fog. Let us spell the issue out more carefully, examining to begin with what language consists of.

The elements of a language are words. What, then, is a word? A word is, to say the least, made up of simple units of speech sound called phonemes—"cat" has three, two consonant sounds and the vowel sound—which combine into a simple phonetic form or syllable called a morpheme. "Cat" is a single morpheme, "caterwaul" includes three.[12] Now, simply to utter the word is to produce the phonemes, in the right morpheme combination, emphasizing or accenting the right morphemes if there are several. To be able to do even just this, pronouncing the word correctly, takes learning and practice; just forming a word orally in a foreign language without a foreigner's accent is a feat, not to mention learning the meaning.

Still, this is quite different from using, and learning to use, the word in sentences (word combinations) in a communicative or expressive act of speech that brings meaning into the picture. To know the use of the word is to know its meaning. And one usually learns this at first in a nonspecial milieu of plain talk, with its mixture of multiple functions and rhythms. Let us think of these, including the familiar meanings, also as components of the language. These, together with the phonemes and morphemes, are its materials.

In this view, language will have a basic sort of "statics." This is the temporal distribution of properly formed phonemes and morphemes into words (vocabulary), together with the grammatically ordered sequence of words in sentences. And there will be a "dynamics" of language, its accents and intervals in word construction and the rhythm of the words in sentences, together with the ways these function or are used in relation to subject matter (meaning), such as asserting, requesting, expressing, and stipulating. This explains why simply uttering a familiar word is like "striking a note on the keyboard of the imagination."[13] It then suggests sentential uses or meanings that are ordered by the informal logic of the language in action, and this logic relates them and makes them subtly compatible or incompatible in various combinations. Thus, uttering a word you know has a keyboard effect, harmonious or jangling.

Once you have learned what something is called—the word or phrase for it—you are prepared to begin putting the word to various uses such as describing the thing, praising it, cursing it, or requesting it. The meaning of the term is realized in such linguistic acts. Thus its meaning is not simply the thing it names or stands for. It is rather what you do with the word or phrase, what sort of linguistic action

[12] Leonard Bloomfield, *Language* (New York: Holt, Rinehart & Winston, Inc., 1956), pp. 79, 161–62.
[13] Ludwig Wittgenstein, *op. cit.*, p. 4.

you take with it, after you have found out that it is what the thing is called.

Such action is usually taken with reference to things as subject matter, about which something is done with the employment of language. Then the language is not "idling" (Wittgenstein). It is coping with things, in working connection with them. This sort of operating on subject matter with words may continue even when the subject matter does not confront you in perception; that is, when you are imagining oɪ thinking about it in its absence. Even then you are using language, perhaps silently, for the sake of something outside the linguistic formulation itself. Most of us do this most of the time.

But suppose one forms phrases for the sake of the verbal resonance, for striking notes on the keyboard of the imagination. What does this involve? Plainly a sort of disuse, if "use" is to have the above sense of action on, and with, subject matter. One who has mastered the language can deliberately get language out of that gear and can *present* things for imaginative prehension in the dynamic medium of the language itself, instead of using the language to *refer* to them as subject matter outside. But this is to mention the content and medium of literature, and so far we have been concerned with the material. How do we get to the medium from here?

We have said that the material is fundamentally the words and sentences with their statics and dynamics learned in nonspecial situations. Statics involve speech sound patterns. Some of these are more sonorous than others. The sonority will be noticed by the word artist and enhanced in various word combinations, which will also be arranged to make certain phonemes more impressive by, say, alliteration, consonance, and rhyme. Thus will the tonal qualities of the language be played up, and the tonal values are a part of its *medium*. The language in this respect is to be intoned, not simply pronounced correctly.

Such intonation, however, brings also the dynamics of the language into play. This is partly an affair of the accents, intervals, or more generally of rhythms. The rhythmic pattern may be made metrical wherever that sort of regularity helps. So we get poetic meter, and all this, together with the tonal values of the statics, realizes the musical qualities of the language. Composing with this in view, the poet is simply a musician whose medium is not just the sonority of tones in a scale but of metered speech sounds. It is this and only this that one gets in listening to a poem in a language he does not know.

What is left out is, of course, the meaning; and I had this in mind before when I spoke of the poet's using meter "if it helps." Some formalists in literary aesthetics talk as if the meaning is a minor, even dispensable, consideration. ("It's not what you say as a poet that counts, it's how you say it.") This makes poetry indistinguishable from music. That consequence is a *reductio ad absurdum* of the formalist's thesis. Of many a musical composition it is rather inept to ask what it means. But not of a literary composition, even if it is an *avant-garde* poem. The reason is that the materials and medium of poetry are linguistic, and "meaningless language" is worse than a paradox. (But this is not to deny that language may mean in different ways.)

Familiar meanings of words are also included in the materials of language. Thus the notion of materials needs to be sharpened and qualified, particularly in relation to the art of poetry.

Just uttering a word, simply performing this locutionary act, is doing a part of what you did with it when you *used* it in the various sayings of real-life situations, where these linguistic acts themselves—denying, explaining, commending things, and expressing feelings—were in turn continuous with the other nonlinguistic activities to which the sayings were instrumental. (You love someone and take action about it, for example, implementing this with familiar speech as you go.) Just uttering a familiar word has a dynamic continuity with all these other activities; and by virtue of this continuity, the word has the power to suggest them, to produce an accompaniment of images, feelings, and dispositions. This suggestion of a network of activities amounting sometimes to a whole "form of life" (Wittgenstein) is built into the dynamics of the language as a part of its material. Anyway, it is this phenomenon I have in mind when I say that familiar meanings are included in the materials of the literary art. This, from the viewpoint of the would-be poet, puts a premium on the rhythms of language, which are conterminous with the dance of life. This accounts for the fact that poets—Paul Valéry, for example—will frequently *first* sense a rhythmic pattern that is curiously meaningful before the phrases are found and becomes fully articulate only in the verse that satisfies it. The poet's own satisfaction is subordinate to that of the rhythmic pattern. A poet is one whose sensitive mastery of the language equips him to satisfy such demands, whose rapport with the language is the sort that allows the language to be master on occasion.

Now, the *medium* of poetry comprises not only the sonorities of the language from the side of its statics, but also what has just been mentioned as the accompaniment of the dynamics of its familiar use: feelings, images, and dispositions. These, together with the sound values of the words, supply the poet with the "color" necessary to the word portraiture which is his art. With an eye to these elements, together with the sound patterns, the literary artist manipulates his linguistic materials like the painter working with his pigments with a prehensive eye to their values in various combinations.

So we get to the content of the poem. This is better understood if we approach the poem, not from the side of material and medium, but from that of subject matter, its theme. Remember, this is as such not a part of the poem. Take, for example, Blake's poem "London." Blake hated London. His hatred and its object, London, are the subject matter of his poem. This is not in the poem as subject matter, but when he composes with language, the medium of the poem is animated with the dynamic image and the feeling. This is, if you like, still the hated London, but now as content of the poem, where fierce verbal action is taken on it in a consuming expressive portrayal of London in the medium of the work. This content, formulated in the medium, is submitted to the rhythms and resonances of the language, where it is at the mercy of their poetic action. Thus, instead of expressing his personal hatred by destructive nonverbal action on the hated thing, he presents the thing as content of a poem and turns the whole passion of hatred loose on it, formulated, activated, and itself presented in the linguistic action of the verse, vis-à-vis the hateful features of the subject matter enhanced as content of the composition. The poem is thus by no means simply a venting of the poet's own passion. It is an expressive portrayal employing special materials, medium, and form to present a subject matter (including the feeling) as content for prehensive vision or aesthetic experience. In short, it is a work of art.

A word here about Langer's notion of the "form of a feeling" (see p. 70). A poem's power objectively to formulate feeling is fundamentally more an affair of activity than of form. The dynamics of language that the poet selectively composes with are, we have seen, continuous with its familiar uses, which themselves attend and interpenetrate many nonlinguistic actions that we engage in or simply experience as spectators. It is this connection that makes certain poetic expressions so powerful and profound, and makes the poem an occasion for half-conscious rehearsal of so many moving experiences. The rhythm of a good poem is the verbal concentration of the rhythms of living and dying.

Metaphor is a moot issue especially in literature, though the concept has itself long been given a metaphorical twist that extends it through all the arts, religion, and metaphysics. Speaking of "metaphorical twist," that is the title of an excellent essay that covers the ground of disputes about metaphor in poetry.[14] Beardsley prefers the "verbal opposition" theory to the "object comparison" theory because

---

[14] Monroe Beardsley, "The Metaphorical Twist," *Philosophy and Phenomenological Research*, XXII, No. 3 (March 1962), 293–307.

the former does greater justice to the way the poet composes with a view to the evocative powers of the linguistic medium. He gets the expressive portrayal by juxtaposing words in unusual combinations that realize new values in medium and content, much as the painter realizes the potentialities of the medium from the side of pigmented materials and of the content from the side of subject matter, by creative juxtapositions that appear discordant or senseless to one not perceptive in the mode of prehension.

The "object comparison" theory, says Beardsley, tempts one to read things into the composition that are not to be found there in its content. If, however, one keeps in mind the distinction between objects as subject matter and objects as content, there may be at least an implicit comparing of objects dissimilar in the nonaesthetic view of them, a comparing suggested by striking or novel juxtapositions of objects as elements of the *content* of the poem. Perhaps this way of construing metaphorical expression—that is, as oriented both toward subject matter and implemented by the verbal opposition that features the linguistic medium—is best on the whole. It has some bearing on Beardsley's rather vague notion of how, in a metaphor, a property is converted into a meaning.

A final remark on the prose forms of the literary art, short stories and novels. (Plays have been considered with dramatic art, though the best of them are certainly literature too.) With stories and novels, the dynamics of language, its phrase cadences and functions, are liberated for the work of presenting subject matter as content, not so much by selectively featuring language and working on its materials as does the poet, but rather by the presupposition that language in such cases is not "working," that it, is not being used in reference to, or in gear with, things simply as subject matter. Just understanding this puts one in a position to watch the story unfold, as content formed in the language medium by the action of the words and sentences. If language did not occasionally "idle" in this controlled way, there would be no art of literature.

We have said nothing about symbols as content of literature, such symbols as those of fertility, death, and evil. The reason for the omission is that this is not the job of the philosopher of literature. It belongs to the literary critic, the historian (Panofsky, for example) and the psychologist. The philosopher's task is confined pretty much to the analysis of categories; in this case, "content" as a category in the language of art criticism.

THE LOGIC

OF TALK ABOUT ART

4

Description of art Talk about art occurs in quite a variety of logically different modes. The general classification that usually gets recognition presents three of these modes: description, interpretation, and evaluation. One can, without too much violence, put most talk about art under one or another of these heads, with some talk overlapping or on the borderline. These functions are logically or conceptually distinct, though actual remarks in the language of aesthetic talk will generally function in more ways than one, sometimes even simultaneously; "good," for example, may have at once a normative and a descriptive meaning. But even such common cases do not destroy the logical distinction betwen the various uses.

There is, however, a deficiency in this threefold scheme. It leaves out expressive portrayal which strictly is neither just description nor just interpretation nor just evaluation, taking each of these in its technically restricted sense. However, if "description" is given a subtle extension, expressive portrayal falls under it, as we shall see. The logic of expressive portrayals is quite crucial for philosophy of art. This point will be developed in this section which, after all, I call description, and in which I treat a number of distinct concepts under that general head.

This whole question of the logic of talk about art I have postponed till the end, to make room first for consideration of art itself. It has recently become the fashion to minimize the discussion of art in favor of the logic of the language of art criticism. And one must grant that talk about art itself is indeed perplexing, often just florid and flamboyant—purple is the word—enough to incline anyone seriously concerned with understanding art to turn hungrily to the logical considerations of sense-making in this area. So to by-pass the logical question entirely would be a sad mistake. A complete phenomenology of art will include both sorts of considerations. This is the best way to take both the false colors and the dreariness out of aesthetics.[1] The sort of question dealt with in this last chapter is nicely illustrated in Frank Sibley's essay,[2] which is typical of the new emphasis on linguistic considerations in current aesthetics.

What is a work of art? This question may be understood as a request for a general description or for a definition. Attempts to answer the question on either interpretation show what an elusive thing the concept of art is. I have avoided the problem till now, since anything like an answer takes shape only after a careful examination of how the term "art" is used. In short, this treatment belongs in this section on the logic of talk about art.

Wonderful test cases to try the adequacy of the answer are to be found among the famous forgeries. The reader is urged to read about the cases of Dossena (statuary), and Wacher and Han van Meegeren (painting).[3] The world's greatest connoisseurs, employing microscopic, X-ray, and acid tests, besides their knowledge of styles and techniques of the original master artists, were at first deceived by the imitation. Shall we say that a forged Vermeer or Van Gogh that passes such tests is not a great work of art, or even that it is not a work of art at all? Something in the concept of art tempts one to say yes to both questions, but there is something else in it that makes a negative reply plausible. One may say that such cases at least try one's concept of art by forcing a consideration of such questions as how X's being a (great) work of art depends, if at all, on its being the work of a particular person, or on simply being thought to be.

But perhaps the art forgeries are too much like counterfeit money to reveal what is more usually troublesome about the concept of art. A perfectly counterfeited dollar bill is as good as a real one with respect to its value, what you can buy with it. If the counterfeit is detected, it becomes worthless on legal grounds alone. Moreover, the *concept* of a dollar bill, and of a "good" one, is crisp enough. Though the legality factor operates in the counterfeit art cases as well, it is more perplexing why a work of art should become relatively worthless if the forgery is discovered, since the value of art is intrinsic, or is commonly thought

[1] See the essay by John Passmore in William Elton, ed., *Aesthetics and Language* (New York: Philosophical Library, Inc., 1954), Chap. 3.

[2] "Aesthetic Concepts," *Philosophical Review*, LXVIII (October 1959), pp. 421–50.

[3] Frank Arnan, *Three Thousand Years of Deception in Art and Antiques* (London: Jonathan Cape, Ltd., 1961).

to be, while the value of money is wholly extrinsic or instrumental, fixed by legal and economic conditions.

Before going on to the aesthetic considerations, let me tease you with the assertion that a perfect imitation of a work of art is, by hypothesis, aesthetically as good as the original. If, knowing it is a perfect imitation, we are not willing to pay anything like the price for it that we offer for the original, it is because the latter has, in addition to its aesthetic value, the value of a close relation to a famous person. It is for this sort of value that people pay enormous sums. This is exactly the kind of value that, say, a bed—any bed—that Napoleon's Josephine slept in has. Similarly, any painting or sketch by Michelangelo, no matter what its merits on aesthetic grounds are, is going to be fabulously priced. Now, back to aesthetics.

The usual perplexity arising around the question, is this a bona fide work of art? is therefore not logically of the sort that might accompany the question, is this a real dollar? Recently the difference has been stated in terms either of various nondescriptive uses, examined below, of the term "art" or of the open texture of the concept, or of both. This is now commonly supposed to distinguish "art" from, say, "dollar bill," since the latter is used as a sort of condensed description of members of a kind of coinage, rendering the concept definable by reference to certain characteristics recognized as necessary and sufficient conditions for X's being a dollar bill, or as the criteria for calling it one. It is such a descriptive use that makes a demand for definition of the term relevant and answerable, and it is precisely on this count that the term "art" is of a different logical stripe. One is perplexed if he tries to use it simply as a descriptive term like "dollar bill." He then attempts a definition, and proceeds to say some pretty arbitrary things, encountering a curious sort of disagreement with other theorists who similarly are seeking the essence or defining characteristics of art and are trying to formulate these in a definition.

The difficulties invariably encountered by this procedure suggest first that the term "art" must be a vague one, like "happiness." And the people who succumb to this suggestion are generally prepared to wait in the expectation that, given more time and effort, the matter will be cleared up by the eventual disclosure of the essence.

But according to the dominant train in current thinking about the problem, this involves the "essentialist fallacy," or the supposition that all works of art have in common an essence or essential quality that is the core of the connotation of the term "art." (See Chapter I, Elton's *Aesthetics and Language*.) This is, in effect, to mistake "art" as a descriptive term, and it motivates the quest for that will-o'-the-wisp, the definitive, general description of anything that is properly called a work of art.

Let us then glance next at the current notion of open-textured terms, among which Morris Weitz classes "art." [4] The term "open texture" is due to the late Friedrich Waismann.[5] He says that open texture characterizes most empirical terms, and that this characteristic, unlike vagueness, cannot be remedied by giving more accurate rules, since open texture is related to the essential incompleteness of empirical concepts. It is a sort of permanent possibility of vagueness belonging to such concepts.

It is this notion that is put to use by Weitz in his account of the concept of art. Thus does he explain its shiftiness. But to go about it this way leaves the concept among empirical descriptive ones, and it was mainly Weitz's purpose to redeem it from such an interpretation, in favor of a nondescriptive one. He proceeds to this, his real point, by bringing in the notion of honorific definitions that use the value-charged term "art" in applications to those features of works of art that the theorist approves of and wishes to celebrate by such honorable mention. Thus most definitions of "art" are verbal acts of featuring and praising the form, or the feeling, or the expressiveness of art works, though these linguistic acts are disguised as general definitions that seem to get at (describe) the essence. This notion of persuasive definition is due to Charles Stevenson, who argues that some terms get charged with emotive meaning.[6] This is to say that they dispose people to direct feelings of approval or disapproval on anything the terms are applied to. "Art" has an aura of such meaning. Like background music, it favorably disposes one toward anything that is put in its sphere of influence. Emotively charged words have the power to do that by a sort of psychological contagion or conditioned-reflex principle. Thus to say with the formalist, for example, that art is primarily or essentially significant form (Clive Bell or Roger Fry) is in effect to feature form by placing it in the warmth of approval generated by the term "art."

But this emotivist account of the nondescriptive meaning of "art" has been pretty much superseded by another nondescriptivist account, one which has influenced Weitz more than has the emotivist. This involves the notion of performative meaning of some utterances.[7] Ac-

---

[4] Morris Weitz, "The Role of Theory in Aesthetics," *Problems in Aesthetics* (New York: The Macmillan Company, 1959), pp. 145–56.

[5] Friedrich Waismann, *loc. cit.*

[6] Charles Stevenson, *Ethics and Language* (New Haven: Yale University Press, 1944), Chap. 9.

[7] J. L. Austin, *Philosophical Papers* (Oxford: The Clarendon Press, 1961), Chap. 10.

cording to this view, some terms are used in linguistic acts of commendation, and this is their whole meaning. Thus the way they function does not involve naming, designating, or describing. This is what is meant by calling them nondescriptive terms. For example, suppose you want to commend something to somebody. Well, you perform the act of commending by saying it is good. "Good" here does not denote any quality of the thing in question. Rather, the term has been forged as an instrument with which linguistic acts of commendation are to be performed. This is its performative meaning—more specifically, its commendatory meaning, a virtue it may possess without the emotive impact which emotivism featured. Many value terms function this way, it is now commonly held, and the point here is that "art" means in some such way, whatsoever descriptive meaning it may also acquire in context by a special and sometimes arbitrary stipulation. To say that "art essentially is y"—form or emotion for example—is thus to commend works of art in which y is present. Then any composition in which this y factor is noticeable at all would qualify simply as a work of art, possibly a bad or poor one. This use of "art" would be partly a descriptive one by means of which something is identified as a work of art. The honorific or commendatory use of the term comes into play when the purpose is to make the y factor conspicuous under the right controls. Taking this as the essence of art in a stipulative definition, "art" is being used to confer favor on and guide choice in the direction of compositions in which this y factor is salient.

Logical analysis of the use of "art" reveals, therefore, that it is inept to treat the word as if it *generally* stands for an essential quality or set of such, presumed to belong definitively and objectively to all works of art. The ineptitude of this treatment is revealed by the discovery that no necessary and/or sufficient conditions can be found for the application of "art."

This is the short story of the shift among recent philosophers of art from the question, what is the essence of art and its real definition? to the question, how is the term "art" used? Such a transition does not abandon the notion of there being good, objective reasons for recognizing something as a work of art. Indeed, it stresses this idea, as against emotivism. Something's being expressive in a certain way, or its exhibiting significant form, is a good reason for calling it a work of art. The traditional mistake occurs only when one or another of these characteristics is alleged to be the defining property of all works of art, and denoted by the term "art."

Of course, what would make, say, realism or feeling or form a good "objective" reason for recognizing something as a work of art would be a certain cultural ethos of the period. Within such a reference frame, some such features would count as the standard in a general way. And it is this that the *avant-garde* artists and critics would deliberately neglect in favor of another emphasis which, if successful, would initiate a new period, another aesthetic ethos. The spirit of the present trends in art seems influenced by, and to influence, the new notion above that "art" is not to be defined *sub specie aeternitatis* or with a view to the eternal essence, so there is a complete and even bewildering freedom of creation, with little concern about previous art forms as standards. Thus, if an appeal is now to be made to good reasons for aesthetic judgment, including just recognition of something as art, these must be of a very special sort, not at all generally applicable as necessary and sufficient conditions.

In fact, these good reasons are so special that they frequently appear as unique features built into the work of art in question for *educated* perception or taste. Without this kind of perceptual sophistication, one cannot see the reasons and, *a fortiori*, whether they are or not good ones. For example, consider the following aesthetic judgment made of Cézanne: "He was at once an incomparable colourist, boldly architectural in his composition, and . . . inventor of the most strikingly new rhythms." [8] With very little paraphrasing this becomes a fairly general description of the paintings for which he is now famous. Let us for the present ignore the evaluative overtones of the judgment—"incomparable," "strikingly new"—to keep it on the level of a descriptive statement, and apply it to, say, his "Still Life with a Plaster Cast" (National Museum, Stockholm; see plate in Raynal, *op. cit.*, I, 49). Now, we want the reasons for the judgment in this particular case. Plainly, these must be something we can see in the painting. Well, anyone can see in it a little statue and fruit and tapestry on a table, and a chest or buffet in the background. None of these is, just like that, any reason for describing the painting as sculptural or architectural, or as vibrant with color rhythms. The list of items is nothing but a specification of the subject matter of the picture. It does not characterize its content or form or medium at all. A simple nonaesthetic looking at the picture is sufficient to corroborate the list. This is to look at the picture simply as a reminder of things to which the figures in the picture are in some respects perceptibly similar, or what it is about.

But an aesthetic judgment featuring architectural and rhythmic characteristics is to be grounded, if at all, still by looking at the picture, of course, but in a different way. If one cannot see, say, the space of the picture as determined by color relationships—what

[8] Maurice Raynal, *History of Modern Painting* (Geneva: Skira International Corp., 1949), I, 47.

we have called first-order form in aesthetic space—he will simply not get the sense of "sculpting or molding by color," or "architectural in composition." And if one is blind to structure in this sense, he will also miss the composition's figured color rhythms, its "motifs," for what this means to painter and critic. The latter are more clearly exhibited by Cézanne's "The Twisted Tree," where his characteristic solidity of composition is not so conspicuous. So even in passing from one work to another by the same artist, aesthetically educated perception will notice "essential" differences, if that term is to be retained and have meaning.

Thus does one *see* the characteristics which count as reasons grounding aesthetic judgments, at the basic descriptive level of talk about art. The important point emerging out of this consideration is that even the bedrock data of art are accessible only to one who can look at things, including works of art, in the relevant way. I have called this way "prehension," distinguishing it from "observation." But this point, though crucial, is tedious beside another associated one that is closer to the theme of the logic of art talk; this is the concept of expressive portrayal in words, at the level of what passes for descriptive talk about art. In short, even description of art is a form of expressive portrayal. It is the logic of this that I want to consider next, briefly, beginning with a nonaesthetic example.

Suppose someone is verbally describing to you the imagery he is having, or had the night before in a dream. What is the logic of such talk? One thing seems clear: you don't suspend your judgment about the truth of the speaker's statement until you can look at what he is talking about, as you might had he asserted that the volume of the block of ice in your ice-box is a hundred cubic inches. Talk about images seems not to refer to *anything* in quite that way. It is talk about impressions of the speaker, and these are not things to be objectively examined *even by him* before he can tell you of them. He simply "has" and reports them. The telling in such cases is, rather, an expressive verbal portrayal of the sort that for him makes the demand for verification nonsensical, while the truth criterion for you, the listener, is his say-so. Nothing in this case is to be more carefully looked at by either of you to make sure. Or let us say that he "shows" you his image in a verbal expression which, as such, does not have to correspond to some nebulous entity inside him which only he can see. Such a notion breeds hopeless and artificial epistemological puzzles. If you really have mastered the living language, it is as if you get the reported image in the pattern of words. This is what "showing" you amounts to in such cases.

Now in the aesthetic case, there is still imagery and feeling involved, but there is a crucial difference. In this case, one is having the impression or image, not just subjectively or in his mind, but in the medium of a material thing perceived as an aesthetic object. So this time it is not just *his* image. In such a case, two or more people may in principle have the same image by prehending the same material thing, by seeing it as an aesthetic object and (subordinately) as this or that subject matter in aesthetic space. One might even speak properly of "objective impressions" in such cases, distinguishing them from the "free" or "floating" impressions of subjective experience.

Suppose, this time, that the structural solidity of the Cézanne composition—which spawned the later cubism—dawns on you as you look prehensively at the picture. You get this impression, and report it in words. Your companion says that the realistic fruit by Chardin or Fantin-Latour is more obviously solid, adding that Huysmans was right about there being some defect in Cézanne's vision. Your problem then is to show him what you mean by the solidity realized through sculpting with color, not by representational realism. How would you do it? By an ostensive definition that involves pointing? Well, in a way, yes; you may, while speaking use your hands in gestures comparable to those of the painter applying the paint, to draw attention to what protrudes and what is recessed by the color arrangements. But it is a property of the medium, not of the material, of the composition that you are talking about. In short, you are trying to convey an objective impression in an expressive portrayal. The very words in this use function somewhat like the pigments under Cézanne's employment. He arranged these pigments with a view to realizing, in the medium of color space, solidity as he saw it, and to making you see it that way. The verbal characterization of the result implements this in the same mode of expression. Comparison with other works where the characteristic in question is more prominent may help; take, for example, the skirt in "Madame Cézanne" (Boston Museum of Art). If, finally, your companion ejaculates about the latter, "How like the face of a cliff of rock!" and, looking back at the fruit, says, "Now I get it!" then the criterion has been satisfied for both of you "having the same objective impression."

This procedure is unlike my describing to you, say, a beetle in my box, and ascertaining whether it is like the beetle in your box (Wittgenstein). Beetles are things, and things may in principle be exhibited in a way that *impressions* of things cannot, howsoever objectively realized in art works the impressions may be. Thus is the logic of the portrayal of impressions different from that of the portrayal of things. And the difference is not to be construed as entailing the incommunicability of impressions. One is tempted to this mistaken conclusion only if one holds up the model of talk about things for talk about impressions of things. And talk about art is included in the latter, the logic of which is the logic of expressive portrayal.

Instead of "solid" in its aesthetic use we might have picked "insipid," "balanced," "flat," "warm," "discordant," "condensed," "economical," or "florid," and made the same sort of point about them, as terms of expressive portrayal grounded by what we have called prehensive perception. It is noteworthy that learning to perceive this way and to use such terms in its light—capacities that develop and mature concurrently, the seeing and the talking—ushers one into an understanding also of the key terms of the language of the philosophy of art: medium, content, form. These also are descriptive terms, though more general ones, in verbal expressive portrayals: the form that is not simply the shape of materials but the order of medium or content; the content that is not simply subject matter; the medium that is not simply material. To understand such terms is to have learned the use of such terms as "dynamic," "balanced," and "warm" in expressive portrayals of works of art.

The critical point is that such terms may be logically primitive in much talk about art, meaning that they are not to be elucidated by other still more elementary terms. You must *see* what grounds the expressive portrayals in which they occur before you can even begin a line of significant talk about art or understand another's utterances in that mode of expression. This is the bedrock of descriptive art talk.

Sibley suggests that the foundation of such talk lies beneath the level both of aesthetic perception and the aesthetic concepts used to express it. "Balanced," "dynamic," and other such terms are primarily literal terms, first learned as such; they later acquire aesthetic significance by a metaphorical transference or extension. This tempts one to think that when one takes to using terms in descriptive talk about art, he gets above perception proper and cannot, strictly speaking, appeal any longer to it for elucidation because his talk has become metaphorical. Yet, as we remarked earlier, Sibley does say that he is concerned with a special "ability to *notice* or *discern* things," which seems to bring some mode of perception back into the picture, as a ground for aesthetic judgment. (He was, in that essay, interested also in evaluative terms, the grounding of which does indeed raise further questions about the relevance of a perceptual foundation. The consideration of this comes later.[9])

I began this discussion of description with the question, what is art? to create an occasion for an account of the meaning or use of "art" and other cognate terms in descriptive talk about art. My suggestion

[9] Frank Sibley, *loc. cit.*

first was that such terms have a nondescriptive use, implying that attempts to give a definition or even a general description are inept. Then I suggested a concept of expressive portrayal that allowed for description of a special sort, with its own logic. I conclude this discussion with something like a general definition of a work of art, after all. A work of art is a material thing produced for prehension as an aesthetic object. This by itself is a rather empty notion, which however gets some substance in connection with the previous treatment of the materials, medium, content, form, and subject matter of a work of art, together with what has been said about prehension as the aesthetically relevant mode of perception of things. As one or more of these items is subtracted or minimized in a particular work, the application of "work of art" becomes more questionable. And not just by *my* stipulation. People, including artists themselves, become less sure. Just one example: take a mobile of parts of a junked car wired together. Even the concept of materials is staggered here, to say nothing of the other four items. The materials of an art are *prepared* for the composition, even in sculpture, or else they are just raw matter. Such a construction seems therefore to lack even material. Along with this goes the puzzlement about the medium and the form. (It might acquire a semblance of these if the arrangement induced one to see it as something, say, a dinosaur, which would give it content. Otherwise you have just shape.)

Moreover, this concept of a work of art has advantages over others, such as the concept that a work of art is a "proposition" [10] or an inner "intuition" [11] or even an "aesthetic object." We certainly hang some works of art on walls but we never hang aesthetic objects or intuitions or propositions on walls. Fundamentally, works of art—even poems— are material things of various sorts. (I did not say "physical objects.") Also, my definition allows for good and bad works of art.

But I do not intend this final flourish to accomplish anything really, or to undercut what has been said about the nondescriptive uses of terms in talk about art.

Let us now step beyond description of art to its interpretation.

Interpretation of art   Actually, description, interpretation, and evaluation are interwoven in live talk about art, and there it is a delicate job distinguishing them. But for philosophy of art it is possible to make some useful distinctions in view of some real logical differences in the living language. So we picture description at the base, grounding inter-

[10] D. W. Sherbourne, *A Whiteheadian Aesthetic* (New Haven: Yale University Press, 1961).
[11] Croce, *Breviary of Aesthetic* (Houston: Rice Institute Pamphlets, 1915).

pretation, which is on the next level up, and evaluation, which is on top. Thus the examination of the logic of interpretive talk about art comes next, in the ascent from the ground of aesthetic experience and its description, up to the sky of evaluative considerations of its formulation in works of art. (Metaphysically viewed, interpretation is perhaps on top, overarching and providing criteria for evaluations, but in the logical view, critical valuation is the most ethereal because its logic is the most elusive, and the philosopher of language considers that sort of thing on top of the hierarchy.)

One must distinguish between the demand for an interpretation of art in general on the one hand, and of a particular work of art on the other, though in practice the two considerations are often not kept separate. The former involves questions not only about works of art but also about aesthetic experience and all its implications. This emphasis naturally results in general speculative philosophies of art, the partisans of which tend to interpret every work of art in the light of overarching universal principles. Of such interpretations there are three sorts: psychological, metaphysical, and theological. Since this way of interpreting art is at present not the fashion, at least in the Anglo-American community, I shall consider it but briefly, together with the logic of such talk. The purpose is to present a few tidbit samples for quick comment, before moving on to the sort of questions about the logic of interpreting that are closer to the art critic's concern.

Prominent under the head of psychological are the theories of the depth psychologists Freud and Jung.[12] The root metaphor here is of a depth in which the important factors for art are down out of sight, in the reservoir of the unconscious. For Freud, these are libidinous fantasies which are repressed as one matures, because in conscious adult life acting out such fantasies as killing one's father or sleeping with one's mother would bring reproach and shame. The artist provides occasions in his works of art for people to get such wish fulfillment in a socially safe and sanctioned way. Thus Sophocles in *Oedipus Rex* and Shakespeare in *Hamlet* please people on two levels: the explicit pleasure of the dramatic unfolding of the plot ("fore-pleasure" or "incitement premium") which is a kind of camouflage on the surface, and the relief of the real wants and tensions beneath in the unconscious, kept down by social censorship.

Jung rejects Freud's notion of what is beneath the threshold of consciousness as too individual and too determined by infantile ex-

[12] Sigmund Freud, *A General Introduction to Psychoanalysis* (New York: Liveright Publishing Corp., 1920). Also see Carl G. Jung, *Modern Man in Search of a Soul* (London: Kegan Paul, Trench, Trubner & Co., Ltd., 1933) and selections in *A Modern Book of Esthetics*, pp. 127–54.

periences. He replaces this with the "collective unconscious" of the human race, a deep reservoir of "archetypal images" that well up into the artist's consciousness to become embodied as symbols in his work. This accounts for its profundity and its mysterious power of massive expression.

Theological interpretations work with the opposite metaphor. The meaning of art is from on high, and this accounts for the exaltation in great works of art. Jacques Maritain, for example, speaks of beauty "descending" to irradiate the objects of the senses with the splendor of eternal forms.[13]

Metaphysical interpretation relies less on the basic metaphor of up and down. We have already glanced at Platonism—which does, incidentally, use the metaphor of ascent out of the dark, as does theology —and we have mentioned Schopenhauer in another connection. He interprets art and its experience as an escape from the throes of a cosmic, irrational will which is the ultimate reality, and which in our practical affairs makes slavish and frustrated agents of us. It uses us as instruments for the satisfaction of its blind cravings. That accounts for the futility of our efforts howsoever final, and for the relief of losing our individuality in the contemplation of art forms. Art is a kind of anaesthetic for the will to live.

All three of the above sorts of interpretations of art tend either to neglect the interpretation of particular works of art together with the consideration of their differences, or to force the general account on each special case until the general meaning is discovered in it. This frequently involves some pretty far-fetched suggestions. (Brutus killed Caesar for the love of Rome, so the Freudian finds the mother image as the symbolic meaning of a city, and the father image in its ruler.)

Now what is the logic of such interpretive talk about art? The logical positivists call all such talk metaphysical because there are no verification or confirmation procedures available. According to them, one simply emotes or vents emotions by using language in that deceptive way—deceptive because, unlike poetry, it seems to frame an argument involving true or false assertions. Thus this expressive use is not a portrayal of anything and, like cries and frowns, has no logic at all, though its words are grammatically in the order of declarative sentences.

But perhaps more than that can be said for such metaphysical interpretations, or for what I like in general to call "constructive metaphysics." We have already noticed how a way of looking at things (mode of experience) is assisted by, or becomes penetrating with the

---

[13] "Beauty and Imitation," *Art and Scholasticism*, 1930. Selection in *A Modern Book of Esthetics*, pp. 26–33.

help of, a concomitant mode of expression or manner of speaking (the appropriate "language"). This modifying power of language reaches down even to perceptual levels of experience, to some extent (Waismann). It can modify the way things look, where the things are not appearing as physical objects or the looking does not involve observation. (But even this involves categorial aspection and the language of science.)

Now, it is the purpose of constructive metaphysics to give us "the great visions of philosophy." It is itself a linguistic *art* whose creations are suggested by the other arts as subject matter when it becomes an interpretation of art. In short, it stands to the arts as a musical composition stands to the theme (subject matter), say, of victory, or as a painting to the model. I conclude, therefore, that its logic is the logic of expressive portrayal, and that its materials are the ordinary meanings of abstract terms juxtaposed for the sake of the cosmic imagery (medium and content) that the composition spawns and articulates (form). "Substance," "mind," "matter," and "form" are examples of such terms. The vision of art that such an interpretation gives will be successful or unsuccessful much as a work of art will fail or succeed. Some will "ring truer" than others, or will be equally adequate in view of different characteristics of the subject matter that are featured and transfigured in the theory, for prehension.

These remarks may suggest that, since abstract terms such as "form," "material," and "content" occur also in my philosophy of art, I too am doing a constructive metaphysics of art. Moreover, some of these terms will not be understood without the help of expressive portrayals at some turns of the exposition. But, clearly, I am not composing these for the sake of a great vision of art in a dramatic, intellectual system. What I am doing is *descriptive* metaphysics of art, or what I prefer to call phenomenology of art and the talk about it. To understand this phenomenological language, one does, indeed, have to be able to see certain things in nonobservational and even nonordinary ways, but not in great visions. The logic of such discourse is the logic of pure, postspecial description, and of expressive portrayal at some points.

Now we get to the issues of interpretation that have greater import to art critics and the artists themselves, as practitioners. The question of interpretation becomes one about the meaning of this or that work of art. I think this question is better paraphrased as, what is one to look for in it? than as, what subject matter outside it does it have a semantic relation to? [14] Frequently, the question of meaning

[14] Monroe Beardsley, *Aesthetics* (New York: Harcourt, Brace & World, Inc., 1958), 319.

can be significantly raised in cases where relation to a subject matter is either lacking or is quite tenuous and unimportant. Moreover, much talk about the meaning of works of art suggests that it is in, or integral to, them. The interpretation should not, in short, get you beyond it to something outside. Of course, it helps to get the meaning if you know what the subject matter is. But even then, what you get will be the *content* of the work when you see the *composition* as the subject matter, or it will be some other ingredient integral to the work if it has no subject matter. So I prefer the question of meaning in the general form: what are we to look for in the work of art?

The question of meaning and the attempts to answer it have often featured the intention of the artist. In fact, some theorists have taken the statement of the artist's intention as an answer to the question. This supposition has been criticized and dubbed the intentionalist fallacy. It is a mistake to suppose that you discover the meaning of the work of art when you uncover what the artist intended to realize in it. As one may say something he did not intend to say, so may the artist fail. Not only this. Even after realizing the discrepancy between what his work "says" and what he intended to say, he may be unable to rectify it to square with his intention, if he is not master of the material of the art. Still more, he may think his intention has been adequately realized in the work, and be shown by objective criticism that it is not, or that a more adequate formulation is feasible by rectifying elements in the composition that "said" something he was not aware of and that negated what he did have in view. All this could happen in language as well. For example, the favorite English translation of Rabelais by Thomas Urquhart simply spills over, beyond the original text, with what Rabelais had in mind; thus it fulfills better the author's intention than his own work did. Thus do the material and the medium have their own powers of expression which may run counter to the intention of the user, depending on how he deploys them.

But, though the meaning is therefore not outside the work of art prehended as aesthetic object, either in the guise of its subject matter or of the artist's intentions, knowing both of these often helps to get at the meaning. This tends to assist one to grasp what is *in* the work, as does an appropriate title.

At this point we are poised to arbitrate a dispute between those two schools of thought about the method of interpretation of art. Let us call "externalists" those who stress the importance of external considerations in the process of interpretation, such as subject matter, intentions of the artist, and historical considerations of his time and person. The "internalists" are those who emphasize the autonomy of the art work, including its meaning, thus requiring that interpretation move within the ambit of the composition itself. The more recent proponents of this view, the New Critics and their practice, the New Criticism, are prominent in the field of the literary art, especially poetry (John Crowe Ransom, Cleanth Brooks, T. S. Eliot, Empson, *et al.*).

A wise arbiter of this dispute will remember that a work of art is mainly for the sake of an expressive portrayal of something, or if not this, then mainly for the sake of some other factor to be prehended in it. We shall see that in the first case, the question of meaning will be primarily about the *content* of the work; in the latter, primarily about the *medium*. In both cases, there will be something outside the work for relevant consideration, though all such considerations will be consummated by a grasp of something in the composition.

If the content is what counts as the meaning and this is in question, then the subject matter, theme, what the work is about, must be considered to answer the question; and these are outside the work. And to ascertain subject matter, it will help to know the artist's intentions, what subject he had in view when he reached for the instruments of this art. Moreover, historical and psychological considerations will throw light on how the subject looked at the time, and how the various media served to articulate it—the symbolism, manners of the period, and other ingredients. Out of all this research will come something that functions like a title for the work or will yield the right interpretation of the title used by the artist himself. Under the influence of such information, the *content* of the work will dawn on the interpreter in a consummatory prehension. The subject matter— emotion, mood, image, situation—will animate the work now as an aspect *internal* to it, as its content. Thus, to have meaning in this way is to have some connection with life or with what is encountered there. Interpretation in this dimension reveals such connections and helps to realize the external life values as internal content of the composition, for aesthetic vision. The arbiter, remembering all this, will also remember to be patient with various interpretations of the same work, in view of the fact that, within limits, it can be seen as different things, as are paintings under the suggestion of different titles, some of which aspects even the artist may have been blind to.

Take *Hamlet* for example. This play accommodates several interpretations. The Freudian interpretation induces one sort of dramatic reading and acting (Olivier's film version), realizing *in* the play (work of art) aspects which, say, a historical interpretation of the new scientific outlook crystallizing in Shakespeare's time would not. One could, instead, see in Hamlet the tragic predicament of a man who senses that the high romance of kingship has been severed from roots in reality and reduced to a mere subjective appearance. There are many evidences of such a "chemical consciousness" in Hamlet. Both interpretations animate the play in view of different themes or subject matters. Or, curiously, one could say conversely that the subject matter gets a special animation, or comes to life, in the work as its content which then seems to be the meaning of the subject matter. In this sense, aesthetic vision finds within art the meaning of ordinary life situations. Who has not had occasion to put it this way in reverse, instead of finding the meaning of art in the life-situations outside it?

So much for the meaning as content.

But if it is the medium, or some property of it, that counts primarily as the meaning—and it must be admitted that this is a more Pickwickian use of "meaning"—then the external considerations that help have to do with the *materials* or instruments of the art work; these also are outside it as aesthetic object, but in an opposite direction from subject matter. (See the chart on p. 36). This is the case in which one is not so much to see the work "as" something, but rather simply to see something "in" it other than content, something that counts as meaning without expressive portrayal. Clear-cut cases of this sort are found in abstract, formal, or nonobjective art.

Suppose, for example, you are listening to Dylan Thomas read his own poem "The Ballad of the Long-Legged Bait" on a recording, and you ask, as you certainly will, what does it mean? This could be taken as a question about content and subject matter, and vague answers could be suggested: oceanic feeling and image of colossal generation, upsurging and abysmal burial. But to press the question in this direction would be to turn your back on what counts perhaps even more, which is the texture of the medium of the composition; and that is what a good interpretation of the poem will draw attention to. How does the interpreter do this? How does he help you to the aesthetic experience of this property of the medium? He reminds you of the *materials* of the poem, not its subject matter. The English language (spoken or heard) is the material, and as material the language is simply the recognizable utterances in grammatical order (secondary material) and the familiar meanings and rhythms of the words together with the usual image or emotive concomitants (primary material). Now, says the interpreter, see what you can do with this material. You juxtapose certain elements in a way that enhances rhythms, sonorities, and alliterations in the secondary material, a way that requires you to go beyond merely pronouncing the words correctly to intoning them, while it freshens the meanings and their ordinary values in the new combinations, metaphorical and otherwise. Thus does the *medium* of the poem emerge for notice, out of the linguistic matrix or base of its *material*. Resonant images and feelings in a volume of significant sound, an aesthetic space textured with these. Dylan Thomas was primarily concerned to compose in his poem this rich texture, to make you see and love the medium of his art. You get the meaning if you get this. And it is *in* the poem, as in a verbal dance.

Of course, one tends also to prehend all Life and Death as *content* of the work in a vague way. This also counts, but as "meaning" in the other sense, contributing to the over-all significance of the poem. (This is true of most good works of art; whichever emphasis is made, both count to some degree.)

One thinks of paintings as having a strikingly similar purpose: for the sake primarily of color texture, a space for the sake of color rhythms and resonances, exhibiting the naked medium of the art by virtue of its specially controlled material—the medium without the dress of content. Think also of abstract music and sculpture in this vein, if you want to get the meaning.

Besides texture there are the form, rhythm, and other elements that may be featured in a more abstract way, minimizing the sensory values of the medium, values of the sort exhibited in the poem by Dylan Thomas. Sometimes an artist will do a work that features these as properties simply of the *material*, and then the interpreter has a less delicate job of showing to do (some mobiles, for example). Where a medium is involved as primary, the interpreting will look beyond the aesthetic object to the material outside, for the sake of revealing the medium internal to the work as aesthetic object. And the logic of this line of talk about art is the logic of expressive portrayal, involving a good deal of showing—even manipulating—the material, while talking about it in a way that helps the learner to see and hear the medium much as he talks expressively about (external) subject matter if the *content* is to be shown. Thus will he get, if at all, the meaning of that sort of art. Whether he finds it interesting or any good, after the insight into its meaning, is another matter, to be the subject of the next and final consideration.

Let us remember here, however, that in most works of art that are not faddist (this too is a veiled value judgment) such properties of the medium as form, rhythm, and sensory resonance blend with, or are, also properties of the content, so that the distinction between two ways of "meaning" must not be mistaken as identical with the distinction between two classes of works of art.

Evaluation of art   I have before me two prints of Oskar Kokoschka's "Dresden, Neustadt III" (View from the Studio). I say that I prefer the little one because it is not murky; the big print on the office wall is murky. You, looking at the same prints, prefer the big one, though

DRESDEN, Oskar Kokoschka (*Galerie Welz, Salzburg*)

you are half ready to concede that, in a sense, it may be murkier than the little print.

What sorts of agreement and disagreement have we here, and on what grounds? How are such disputes to be arbitrated?

Let us both first look more closely at my use of "murky," since this is plainly the occasion for some hesitation on your part. Is it a descriptive or a value term in this context? "It is murky" could here be either a normative statement (value judgment) or a description. If it simply means that the color values of the big print are uniformly dark and that, by implication, it is uniformly darker than the little print, then you and I can agree on this, though our preferences still differ. The description is confirmed by simply looking at the colors of the material things (prints) before us. But if "It is murky" means "It is *too* dark,"—and this is what I meant to say—then we certainly have a critical assessment of the print, and it is on this count that you disagree with me. The remark on that interpretation is too closely related to my preference, which is in conflict with yours. It then functions, if it is true, as a good or supporting reason for my preference, while unseating yours.

Suppose now the dispute is over this evaluation. Is the large print too dark? You admit that it is darker than the little one, but deny that it is too dark. You are not sure that you prefer it just because it is darker—that, you feel, could be but may not be the reason—but you *are* sure you prefer the darker one. So I begin the defense of my position.

I point out that the space of the picture is not as crisply determined when the colors are so dark. There is still aesthetic space order, to be sure, but I like to know where I am in picture space, and the darker picture leaves the relations of elements in it too obscure for that. I want to be and move in the light of a more determinate milieu. I want this milieu to be as articulate as possible. Moreover, in the brighter print, I see and feel the glazes better, what color covers the color beneath, and the stucco, almost chalky quality that the brightness brings out, especially in the sky above the buildings. I see it as a sky, yes, but without losing the sense of the sculpting with color and the feel of pigment and canvas beneath, transfigured in the medium.

Then it dawns on you why you prefer the darker picture. You agree that this does indeed leave more obscure, or less articulate, the aesthetic orders of the medium, and tends to mute the color resonances of the materials. But it is precisely materials and medium that you want minimized in favor of a softer space for Dresden as content of the picture. This accommodates a more mystical aesthetic experience of the city you love. There is more room in it for the emotion of a lover of the *subject matter* of the composition.

Well, we might thus reach an understanding, if not an agreement. You love the subject matter and I love the medium of the art of painting. And each of us has at least uncovered a reason for his preference, or a justification of his evaluation as too dark or not too dark. We also understand that expression, in a large sense, is the job of art. There is the sort of expression in which the materials of art are transfigured or become articulate in the medium (first-order form and formulation), and then there is the expressive portrayal of subject matter from the other side in the content, where the properties of the medium are subordinated to the transfiguration of the things of ordinary experience (in a second-order formulation). We remember that these two factors are not generally separate in an actual work of art.

So much for the understanding. But the disagreement remains as to which print is better. (Of course, a print is ordinarily judged better or worse according to its faithfulness to the original. Our discussion clearly is not considering its worth simply in that connection. We are in effect arguing as to which would have been the better way to paint the original.) To say simply that this is a relative matter, one print being better for your sort of interest, the other for mine, leaves something unresolved. So I carry the examination further.

It may be that you would prefer even more an off-focus, under-exposed color photograph of the city you love. That too could be an occasion for mystical, emotional response, more satisfying than the dark print of the painting. If such a photograph were not itself taken and processed with some view to the architectonic of color juxtapositions and over-all pattern, I would have ground for suspecting that you prefer the darker Kokoschka mainly because it is serving you as a reminder of the subject matter you love, not as an expressive portrayal of it. If so, you would be overlooking, or would be blind to, the medium, and what is more, to the very content of the picture; and then your preference would be grounded by no artistic considerations at all. Your reasons, when disclosed, would turn out to be irrelevant to any aesthetic judgment.

So there is a residue still of the problem of learning to see what is relevant as a reason for critical judgment of a work of art. Perhaps in this open-textured concept we have a sort of objective control, howsoever elastic, the appeal to which could help us at least to approximate an agreement as to which print is better. Several considerations would count as relevant under this head, and none of them would be a necessary or sufficient condition *in general,* but they would count as good reasons do in art, in context or in this special case.

Looking at the prints this way, after some such education regarding what one is to look for in art, perhaps I would be weaned from a too exclusive concern with medium, materials, and form, a concern of the sort that moved Roger Fry to say that, in art, *what* is formulated doesn't count, only *how* it is formulated. And you might be weaned from an excessive preoccupation with subject matter that neglects, as Tolstoy tended to do, the question as to how this is realized as content of the *composition,* if at all. But there is something sentimental, fatuous, and unrealistic in talking this way. People do not in fact need as much agreement of this sort as is here suggested; nor do artists and the understanding of the arts proceed on the assumption of progress towards such ultimate agreement. Still, we do differ in our evaluations, and give supporting reasons. And this does presuppose some sort of ideal of objectivity and excellence. I think this has its taproot in the concept of art that, for all its open texture and occasional honorific or commendatory use, is nevertheless a *concept,* and one with normative force; not just an instrument for exhibiting personal taste from case to case. In the body of this little book, I have tried to harness this conceptual Pegasus without clipping its wings. The result is an ideal comparable to Ortega y Gasset's: that the greatest art is formally expressive at once of materials on the one hand and of subject matter on the other, doing justice to both in a reciprocal transfiguration, each inspiring the other in the content of the composition. Anyone who gets the point of this condensed remark will have the key to the philosophy of art in this small volume.

Now for a few final, sharper points about the logic of evaluative talk about art. The example of the Kokoschka print displays most of the issues that come up in this connection. But I should spotlight some of them before putting down my pen.

First, a final argument about the Kokoschka example. If the dispute had begun with my saying, "The big print is worse," and you had challenged this, I might properly have supported my evaluation with, "it is too dark," which is *also* an evaluative judgment. This may seem curious from a logical point of view, but it is a phenomenon that frequently occurs in normative discourse about art. Of course, what happens in such legitimate cases is that a lower-order value judgment is made to support a higher-order judgment. The lower-order judgment is supported by a kind of educated looking at the composition in question —"too dark"—which makes an appeal to experience relevant. In short, though it is a critical assessment, it also functions as a description. But what it describes is a datum of prehension or aesthetic experience, the special way of looking that Sibley and others had in mind when they spoke of the critical appreciation that grounds evaluative talk about art. Thus, the lower-order assessments constitute a kind of *normative description* that makes demands on one's powers of perception. Having satisfied this, you may *see* why I say the large print is too dark. And it is this judgment that supports the higher-order evaluation, "It is worse." The latter is not so directly decided by looking, since "worse," unlike "too dark," is not primarily a descriptive term at all. It has performative meaning, and the condemnatory judgment in which it occurs is justified if the lower-order normative description (too dark) is true.

This suggests a teasing thought: "too dark," because it is normatively descriptive, is in this context a value term (negative); "worse" is not. If you can *see* the disvalue denoted by "too dark" in the normative description, you have in view the reason for using "worse" in the condemnation. It is by appeal to the positive or negative values as data of aesthetic discernment (Sibley) reported in normative descriptions that we justify our use of the performative terms "worse," "good," and "better" in commendations or the opposite; and these are not value terms. They are grounded by value terms.

Now, in quick conclusion, I put the spotlight on some other evaluative terms of talk about art to exhibit other facets of its logic.

"Beautiful" has, for good reasons, been discarded by careful critics, on the whole. Even some philosophical aestheticians of the more traditional sort have noticed its liabilities for talk about art. The main reason is that its common—even primary—use is not relevant to aesthetic considerations. "Beautiful" goes along with "lovely," and "lovely" ties in with "lovable." This puts you at the dead center of life situations where you fall in love with things and find them beautiful. Now, the congenital artist is precisely the sort of person who, as such, is not in that sort of relation to things; sometimes he is incapable of it even as a man. One may love—and find beautiful—material and spiritual things and the fusion of these in persons, but to experience these as aesthetic objects, or to portray them expressively in works of art, is to exclude that sort of intimacy with them in favor of another more impersonal sort. To call them "beautiful" in view of such virtues as those that shine forth in this impersonal intimacy is confusing and misleading. Similar remarks hold for "pretty," "charming," and, of course, their opposites.

"Unified," "balanced," "incongruous," "dynamically contrasting," "delicate," and other such terms serve the aesthetic purpose better, mainly from the side of medium and form. Notice, however, that these may function quite naturally as perception terms of what I have just called normative description, so they usually occur in the lower-order evaluations, grounding the final, higher-order performative evaluations that use "good," and "great." In actual art criticism, the latter are often left implicit. Having judged a work of art unified, it is a sort of redundancy to go on to add that it is good art. Nevertheless, the critic should remember tenaciously that he is not giving generally necessary or sufficient conditions of the goodness he leaves unspoken. That kind of deductive logic does not fit the aesthetic case.

Featuring content are such terms as "expressive," "insightful," "revealing," and "profound." These too may function as terms of normative description, making demands on the capacity for the prehensive way of looking; this time, however, in the form of experiencing the composition as the subject matter. And this, in turn, presupposes some perceptiveness of things in real-life situations. You will fully get the content of the work of art only if you are sufficiently impressionable in your ordinary relation to the world. If you are not, you will be among those who do not naturally turn to art for its illuminating "comment" on what people experience. And such art works as you do incidentally encounter will serve you as reminders, not expressive portrayals. You will fail to get their sense; you will miss what is *in them*.

This point may be pressed by noticing some terms of normative description that are still more specific and pertain mainly to content. I heard a well known artist characterize Picasso's "Guernica" as expressing "apocalyptic protest." This is close to being a statement of just subject matter, but pondering it shows not only its interpretive but also an evaluative force. It amounts in a way to a favorable evaluation, or is clearly a good reason for one. Now anyone who has not been perceptive about the unmitigated terror of war for noncombatants at home will be at least partly blind to the content of that powerful picture, there for prehension.

That word "powerful" is a specially significant specimen. It straddles the fence between content terms and form-medium terms. That most of the other terms do this also to some extent is surely clear, after what has been said about the fusion of medium, form, and content in actual art work, but "powerful" cuts across, even after the conceptual distinctions have been made for purposes of art analysis. The reason for this is that "powerful" goes along with "moving," and such dynamic mobility may belong either to the formal rhythms of medium, or to the vitality of the content realized in it, or to both at once.

The consideration of "great," especially in the phrase "great art," will conclude this study of the logic of evaluative talk about art, and so the book. It has some connection with the notion of pure and impure art, if this is construed in a certain way. A work of art may be said to be pure if: (1) it does not combine several arts; opera is impure on this count, combining dramatic action with music and verbal utterance; (2) it does not employ several media; a single art like poetry is impure on this count because it uses the medium of sound and of the evocative meanings of the words; (3) it excludes content from the medium or media whatsoever; any art is impure on this count to the degree that it is representational—an expressive portrayal of any subject matter; and (4) it is not muddied by, or mixed with, nonaesthetic modes of expression; a novel is impure in this sense to the extent that it includes historical reporting or political propaganda or straightforward moralizing, functioning then not as an expressive portrayal, but as a reminder of things, or of things to be done.

So there are purists of different kinds in relation to art, and each will make a different sort of demand. He *recommends* what he means by pure art by calling it "great." For example, the first group will frown on *La Bohème*. The second will prefer Sibelius to Dylan Thomas. The third will prefer Bartók to Sibelius and Ben-Shmuel to Michelangelo. The fourth will reject George Eliot, Dos Passos, and Steinbeck in favor of Thomas Mann and Melville.

By the same token, there will be various kinds of impurists in art, calling "great" the compositions that contain the various mixtures in one or more of the four senses of "impure."

Both purists and impurists of the sorts above tend to "define" art persuasively in the warm glow of such preferences, with a view to what they take to be great art. We have studied the merits and demerits of that procedure.

How might one arbitrate such a dispute? Weitz (see p. 82) has already suggested something in this direction, showing what is achieved for art by various honorific emphases; perhaps that is enough. But I have another supplementary suggestion. Making it requires a more precise consideration of just what it is that is judged great in art.

It is the work of art, to be sure, that is thus judged. But we must make more of certain distinctions. Is it the work of art simply as a material thing—never, of course, as a physical object—or the work of art as aesthetic object, or some performance of the work that, strictly speaking, is being evaluated? Or a property that the work has in relation to something external?

Let us begin with what seems most peripheral to the work, the performance of a work from among the performing arts. *Hamlet* again, for example. When we call *Hamlet* a great work of dramatic art, is it the performances, or some one or a few of them, that strictly and ultimately is what we have in view? Of course, each performance as such can be judged excellent or great, and then the commendation goes to the performers in that instance. But surely it is with a view to what they present or realize in the pattern of the performance that we make even that judgment of greatness. And this has its taproot in the play. This is something written and first to be read. Even the performers read it first, before rehearsal and final performance. And the reading, what does that go back to? To the living language in speech, with all the primary and secondary materials (rhythms, sonorities, familiar meanings) it affords the literary and dramatic composer-artist. If this is not "lived" in the auditory and visual imagination as the play is read, there is no final confrontation with the work of art, which at base is just this material thing, howsoever ethereal or spiritual what it captures may be when the work is prehended as an aesthetic object. This is the bedrock control on what one is to see in the work; it is *the* work of art, the final court of appeal. This, fundamentally, is what is judged in aesthetic assessments of the various levels or orders.

Of course, prehending it as an aesthetic object involves aspection, and this brings the legitimate options or various interpretations into the picture. Still, aesthetic objects, or performances or interpretations featuring the aspects, are not the final consideration in value judgments of the work of art. But they are, in a way, of the essence, since a work of art is a material thing designed for prehension as an aesthetic object. It is not *just* a material thing. It is designed to be an occasion for animation by aspects, in the aesthetic view of it. So we judge it great in proportion to its capacity to function that way, as it presents for prehension the spirit of its materials in the first-order form of its medium, and of its subject matter in the second-order form of its content, fusing these in the third-order form or style of the work as a whole. And how are we to know when such balance and blend is achieved? Deciding this will depend fundamentally on an educated look at the work of art, among other considerations such as the perennial importance of the theme or subject matter for man as man. So, for example, the work of art whose theme is love with its tragic complications will tend, on this count alone, to be greater than one about business success. And the literary art has the biggest potential for greatness among the arts, simply because language is its material and because the form of language is closest to being our form of life. (One talks as he makes love, for example; he does not paint or sculpt.) And the English language, though at present deteriorating at an alarming rate, most closely approximates that coincidence. So works of art in English have the advantage in the art of literature, which is potentially the greatest among all the arts.

The book ends teasingly on this dogmatic note. Whether it rings true or not—"it" may mean either the note or the book—will be explored by the people it intrigues, perhaps even infuriates. Out of the fine fury some good ideas may emerge or, better yet, some good insights.

For

further

reading

Full bibliographies are contained in Rader's *A Modern Book of Aesthetics* and in Beardsley's *Aesthetics*, both mentioned below.

Anthologies

Elton, W., *Aesthetics and Language*. New York: Philosophical Library, Inc., 1954.

Langer, S. K., *Reflections on Art*. Baltimore: The Johns Hopkins Press, 1958.

Margolis, J., *Philosophy Looks at the Arts*. New York: Chas. Scribner's Sons, 1962.

Rader, M., *A Modern Book of Aesthetics*, 3rd ed. New York: Holt, Rinehart & Winston, Inc., 1960.

Vivas, E. and M. Krieger, *The Problems of Aesthetics*. New York: Holt, Rinehart & Winston, Inc., 1953.

Weitz, M., *Problems in Aesthetics*. New York: The Macmillan Company, 1959.

Aesthetic experience

Aldrich, V. C., "Picture Space," *Philosophical Review*, LXVII (July 1958).

Aristotle, *The Art of Poetry* (*Poetics*), trans. Bywater. London: Oxford University Press, 1938.

Beardsley, M., *Aesthetics*, pp. 527–30, New York: Harcourt, Brace & World, Inc., 1958.

Cassirer, E., *Essay on Man*. New Haven: Yale University Press, 1944.

Caudwell, C., *Illusion and Reality*. New York: International Publishers Co., Inc., 1947.

da Vinci, Leonardo, *Treatise on Painting*. London: George Bell & Sons, Ltd., 1897.

Dickie, G., "Is Psychology Relevant to Aesthetics?" *Philosophical Review*, LXXI (July 1962).

Freud, S., *Introductory Lectures on Psycho-Analysis*. London: George Allen and Unwin, Ltd., 1929.

Gombrich, E. H., *Art and Illusion*. New York: Pantheon Books, Inc., 1960.

Jung, C. G., *Modern Man in Search of a Soul*. New York: Harcourt, Brace & World, Inc., 1934.

Knox, I., *Aesthetic Theories of Kant, Hegel and Schopenhauer*. New York: Humanities Press, 1958.

Plato, *The Republic*, trans. Cornford. New York: Oxford University Press, 1945.

Sibley, F., "Aesthetic Concepts," *Philosophical Review*, LXVII (October 1959).

Tolstoy, L., *What Is Art?* London: Oxford University Press, 1930.

Tomas, V., "Aesthetic Vision," *Philosophical Review*, LXVII (1959).

Also: See relevant selections in anthologies above.

A work of art

Arnheim, R., *Art and Visual Perception*. Berkeley: University of California Press, 1957.

Auerbach, E., *Mimesis*. Garden City: Doubleday & Company, Inc., 1953.

Greene, T. M., *The Arts and the Art of Criticism*. Princeton: Princeton University Press, 1940.

Grosser, M., *The Painters' Eye*. New York: New American Library of World Literature, Inc., Mentor Books, 1956.

Hospers, J., *Meaning and Truth in the Arts*. Chapel Hill: University of North Carolina Press, 1946.

Langer, S. K., *Feeling and Form*. New York: Charles Scribner's Sons, 1953.

———, *Philosophy in a New Key*. Cambridge: Harvard University Press, 1957.

MacDonald, M., "Art and Imagination," *Proc. Arist. Society* (1953), 205–66.

Weiss, P., *The World of Art*. Carbondale: Southern Illinois University Press, 1961.

Wittgenstein, L., *Philosophical Investigations*, pp. 193–231. New York: The Macmillan Company, 1953.

Ziff, P., "Art and the 'Object of Art,' " *Mind*, LX (October 1951).

Also: See relevant selections in anthologies above.

The arts

Clark, K., *The Nude*. Garden City: Doubleday & Company, Inc., 1959.

Greene, T. M., *The Arts and the Art of Criticism*. Princeton: Princeton University Press, 1940.

Hanslick, E., *The Beautiful in Music*, trans. G. Cohen. New York: The Liberal Arts Press, Inc., 1957.

Hitchcock, H. R., *Architecture*. Baltimore: Penguin Books, Inc., 1958.

Langer, S. K., *Problems of Art*. New York: Charles Scribner's Sons, 1957.

Newhall, B., *Photography*. New York: Museum of Modern Art, 1938.

Panofsky, E., *Meaning in the Visual Arts*. Garden City: Doubleday & Company, Inc., Anchor Books, 1955.

Raynal, M., and A. Smith, *Exploring Poetry*. New York: The Macmillan Company, 1955.

Valéry, P., *The Art of Poetry*. New York: Alfred A. Knopf, Inc., Vintage Books, 1958.

Wright, F. L., *The Natural House*. New York: Horizon Press, Inc., 1954.

Also: See relevant selections in anthologies above.

The logic of talk about art

Austin, J. L., *Philosophical Papers*, chap. 10. London: Oxford University Press, 1961.

Black, M., ed., *Philosophical Analysis*, chap. 5. Ithaca: Cornell University Press, 1950. Also, *The Importance of Language*. Englewood Cliffs: Prentice-Hall, Inc., Spectrum Books, 1962.

Hampshire, S., "Logic and Appreciation," *World Review* (1952).

Jones, E., *Hamlet and Oedipus*. Garden City: Doubleday & Company, Inc., Anchor Books, 1954.

MacDonald, M., "Some Distinctive Features of Arguments Used in Criticism of the Arts," *Proc. Arist. Society*, Supplementary Vol. XXIII (1949).

Margolis, J., "The Identity of a Work of Art," *Mind*, LXVII (1959).

Sibley, F., "Aesthetic Concepts," *Philosophical Review,* LXVII (October 1959).

Waismann, F., "The Resources of Language," *The Importance of Language,* ed. M. Black. Englewood Cliffs, N. J.: Prentice-Hall, Inc., Spectrum Books, 1962.

Weitz, M., "The Role of Theory in Aesthetics," *Jour. of Aesthetics,* XV (1956).

Ziff, P., "The Task of Defining a Work of Art," *Philosophical Review,* LXII (1953).

Also: See relevant selections in anthologies above.

INDEX

W

Z